MW00874688

The Art of
the Conjure

BARBARA DACA

Copyright © 2017 Dr. Barbara Ann Daca, D.Div.

All rights reserved.

ISBN 10: 1544844689
ISBN-13: 978-1544844688

DEDICATION

To My Sons: Robert and Johnathan, and my Brother Chris; for they know not the depth of the power they hold, and yet it treats them well!
To all the Male Witches at One Pot Witchery: Garret, Seth, Dillon, Kevin, Erik, Hunter, Joey and Zachery, May your lives be filled with the magick you were born to hold! And to our new Witch on the Rise, Anastasia may your journey be blessed and your powers unfold!
And to all the Male Witches the World over , as you hold the Powers of the Gods Within, We Honor you and are proud to Walk Beside You between the Worlds!

FORWARNED:
This book is not going to be like any other hoodoo book you will come across. The Appalachian Mountains run from Northern Alabama, to Newfoundland and Labrador and breaks apart into Greenland, Scotland and the Western Seaboard of Europe, All part of the Ancient Caledonian-Appalachian Mountain Range. It is not strange at all that when the Scots, Celts and Germans sought religious freedom, they crossed an ocean only to land on the west side of the mountain range like their Viking brothers before them. As the vibrations are the same, it called to them, and they heard the mountain's song. Therefore the God's of the Appalachia hail from either the Indigenous Tribes or from the Gods of the North i.e., The Gods of the Vikings and the Druids. When they arrived they sought solace, isolation and kept to themselves. A vacation in the Appalachia means going to the lake, visiting the cousins or going to Grandma's, you really never traveled far away from your kin. Many people growing up in the Appalachia will tell you that until very recently, you never even saw, heard or spoke to anyone that was much different than you. So Appalachian hoodoo, conjure, Granny magick, pow wow etc. didn't live outside of your family, village or neighborhood and so it wasn't influenced by any outside forces. It was the Pennsylvania Dutch that brought over the black chickens and their special brand of Pow Wow medicine; it was the Scot and the Irish that brought over their Cunning Folk, it was the Germans that brought over their Hexe maidens, it was the Scandinavians who brought their Nordic Witchcraft mixed with Sumi Shamanic practices and intertwined it with the Indigenous Medicine Men and Woman. It is from these lands we can trace our Ancestries, our Magick and our Doctoring. These lands that suffered the worst of the Witch Trials and were looking for Religious Freedom. Many interlaced Christianity with charms and we give a nod to these by listing the Psalms and the Saints in the Index. Many others however, only went to Sunday Meeting for the sense of Community it offered. And so most of this book will reference their ways and their gods. For we never bend our knee in supplication to our Gods and Goddesses, Nor do we beg for them to do for us. Rather we ask them to empower us, so that we may do for ourselves – therein lies the Appalachian Way.
For our generations were not born into sin like the Sons of Abraham, our code of ethics clearly states that a person is only as good as their word, and if you give a promise, you are to fulfill it, either in this lifetime or the next. We are also just as likely to curse our neighbor as to bless them. That's just because if we don't bend down to Gods, then we aren't likely to take guff off of people neither. In the words of Odin "Whenever you know of harm, regard that harm as your own; and give your foe's no peace!" -Odin, Havamal 197. So we will regard your harm as our own and act accordingly.

Therefore we can be found putting wolf scat under the barn floor so your cows won't enter just as easily as we can be found bringing over a meal and keeping up chores for you if you become injured. We need also to clearly illustrate another significant difference that came over on the boat to religious freedom with us. Our ancestors have always represented Father Sun with the eight spokes of the Wheel. Meaning there are Eight seasons of the suns passing in a year, not four. They are the Solstices, the Equinoxes and the Cross Quarter celebrations. We know this in our hearts to be true, the Seasons are eightfold. So then I would like you to take a look at the "Solar Cross" and note that it has only 4 points, not eight. I would like you to now imagine it as a Lunar Cross and see the Truth of it. In the Lunar Cross we see our own Four Fold Goddess; The New Moon representing the birth of the Maiden, coming from the darkness of the womb into the light. The Rising Moon representing the Warrior Maiden, as a warrior rises up in battle becoming her full self, so too does the Moon rise. The Full Moon represents the Mother aspect who becomes pregnant and full of life. The Waning Moon therefore represents the Wisdom of the Crone who will wither like the flower and spring up again in the never ending Circle of Life. In your heart of hearts, you see it, you feel it and you know its truth. The Warrior Goddess was stripped from us so we wouldn't rise up, but she wakes from her sleep now, so rise up with her and regain your heritage. Remember it in your breath, in your blood and in your bones, just like in your memories you still envision talking to the snakes and the bees. Appalachian Hoodoo is its own brand of sympathetic magick and conjure, just like handling snakes in church is our own brand of Gospel. Remember a Witch who cannot curse, cannot heal! Be Well Blessed my Brothers and Sisters! Skul!

CONTENTS

ACKNOWLEDGMENTS

All text and content found herein is completely comprised by myself, (unless otherwise acknowledged herein, as in the 5th Century Poetry or Words of Odin) Dr. Barbara Ann Daca, D.Div. and so all rights are reserved by myself, My daughter Cathleen, and One Pot Witchery.

1 BONES & STONES

The Difference between Appalachian Hoodoo and all other hoodoo begins right here on page one, for never in the history of our generations have we ever used roadkill for the purpose of divination. We have always taken our fate into our own hands and slaughtered the animal ourselves or chose it and had it slaughtered specifically for us, or used one who died naturally. This is not to say they are killed just to read the future, as that would be a waste and a disgrace. They are in their turn, slaughtered for food and read accordingly. So when say, a sheep is slaughtered for food, a hip bone may be taken to a seer and the carving marks left on it may be read or burned to divine the New Year. So to us, throwing bones or stones are no different. In fact it is a long held form of Divination as the Skeleton is a symbol of underlying Truth, much like Runes, it is very useful in Divination. However one should go with their roots, as you will be working with your Ancestors. So here we will note that it is the Trickster that was sent to us to teach us our lessons and so it is by the Trickster we divine. Therefore the use of the bones of a Rabbit, Stag (symbolizing the Greenman or Horned God), Crow or Raven (Odin, Hekate, the Morrigan) and the Coyote are best. To help you in your quest for your own set, many Appalachian farms still raise rabbit and hare, for meat and will process the hide for you as well. If you don't hunt, stag horns naturally fall off between the months of January and April and can often be found when out on walk about, as can crow bones. When finding, say a Crow, Raven or Coyote while on walkabout, wear gloves, wrap them up, transport and then bury these respectfully before use. Note again, that none are ever killed solely for the purpose of divination and divination sets do often include stones, coins, stalks, roots, shells, and owl pellets and hosts of other things, as well as bones.

Symbolically, Rabbits not only Strengthen our Intuition but help you receive and interpret Hidden Teachings. Crow or Raven, brings in Magick and a Higher Perspective, giving you the Power of Insight. While Stag brings Guidance, and Connection to Spirit, as well as, Psychic Power. Coyote Reveals the Truth behind illusion and chaos. He will also reveal any deception that is going on in your life. We can see now how these bones will enhance any divinations and connection you have with Spirit. However, before one even considers throwing the bones, one must first get right with their Ancestors, for the bones are divined through their help and influence. Each piece of the set is reflected on and its meaning ascertained through conversations with them. Praying to your Ancestors for guidance and wisdom is highly recommended as they will teach you and guide you into the understanding of each piece and how it relates to the message at hand.

Preparation of the bones is necessary as well. They must be cleaned, dried, blessed and consecrated before use. Sage and incense are often used in this preparation as is hydrogen peroxide for whitening. Sometimes bones are carefully whitened and then colored for easier interpretation. Here are some plants and such you can use for **Natural Dyes:**

For Yellow Dyes: Cumin, Yarrow (will also make green and black), Honey Locust Golden Wild Indigo (will also make green), Yellow Onion Skins, Tall Cinquefoil (will also make black, green, orange and red), Turmeric, Pecan (will also make brown) Indian grass (will also make brown, and green), Chamomile Tea.

For Orange Dyes: Chili Powder, Western Calandra (will also make brown and yellow), Paprika, Prairie Bluets (will also make brown and yellow), Bloodroot (will also make brown and yellow), Carrots, Sassafras (will also make black, green, purple, yellow), Eastern Cottonwood (will also make black brown and yellow), Plains Coreopsis (will also make black, green, yellow and brown).

For Red/Pink Dyes: Red ochre or red brick dust and red wine can be mixed into a paste and then used to redden the bones, Ozark Chinquapin (black, yellow, brown, depending on the part of the plant used), Red Grape Juice, Cranberry, Red Onion Skins, Sumac (also yellow, green, brown, black), Choke Cherry, Prairie Parsley (also yellow, brown), Cherries, Pomegranate, Raspberries, Slippery Elm (also brown, green and yellow), Black Willow (also black, green, orange and yellow).

For Purple/Blue Dyes: Blueberry, Blackberry, Indian Blanket (also black, green and yellow), Hairy Coneflower (also brown, green, yellow, black), Red Mulberry (also yellow, green), Mountain Alder (also brown, red, orange), Purple Cabbage, Red Onion Skins, Red Zinger Tea, Violet Blossoms, Summer Grape (also orange, yellow and black), Black Locust (also black, green, yellow, brown).

For Green Dyes: Butterfly Milkweed (also yellow), Texas Paintbrush (also green, red, yellow), Spinach leaves, Dark Green Leafy Vegetables, Basket Flower (also yellow), Sagebrush (also yellow and green), Stinging Nettle (let set for 2 weeks after cutting to make dye), Goldenrod (also yellow, brown).

For Grey Dyes: Iris (also black), Butternut (also brown), Canaigre Dock (also yellow, green and brown).

For Brown Dyes: Coffee, Dill Seeds, Tea bags (also green, red, yellow depending on the tea), Prickly Poppy (also green, orange, and yellow), Texas Paintbrush (also green, red, yellow), Walnut Shells (also black), Elderberry (also yellow), Downy Phlox (also brown, green and yellow).

For Black Dyes: Northern Catalpa (also brown, yellow), Sumac (also yellow, red, green and brown), May Apple (also brown and yellow), Evening Primrose (also green, orange, red and yellow).

Once they have been made exactly how you desire them to be, they are then presented to the Ancestors with a meaning to establish a language between you and them. If the Ancestors are unknown or not helpful, a Spirit Guide or Power Animal may be used. The bones are then kept in a leather bag or wooden bowl on the Ancestral Altar (or an altar dedicated to your guides). Some practitioners paint or otherwise mark them to help them ascertain their meaning, for instance, if the bone is laying up (favorably) or down (unfavorably) a small dot or line or color may be made at one end. Certain bones or things may have universal meanings but the Ancestors or Spirit Guides ultimately determine the language used between them and you. Therefore, begin by talking to your Ancestors every day. Have conversations with them, ask them questions, ask for guidance and answers. Just before you sleep is a good time to practice as you will naturally receive an answer by morning.

Some Examples of Universal Meanings you may desire to use are:

Front Paw, Ankle Bone or Wing Bone: Travel

Neck Bone: Poverty, stationary, incoming or outgoing

Dice: Add the Numbers and Reduce like Numerology for the essence.

Wish Bone or Left back Rabbits Foot: Desires or Good Fortune

Penis Bone or Stag Antler: Male or Horned God Bone

Rib Bone or Cowrie Shell: Female or Goddess Bone, also Support and Guidance.

Sea Shell: Communication or News.

Buzzard Bone: Illness or Blockage

Breast Bone: Love or the Heart of the Matter

Hip Bone: Fertility, Giving Birth or a Project Forthcoming

Circle, Ring or Round Bone: represents a Cycle, Pivotal Period or Process.

Knee Bone: Flexibility, Humility or Pride.

Horseshoe: Luck, both good and bad, sudden change, the unexpected

Nails or Claws: Search for something that has been Hidden.

Finger or Hand Bone: Primary Skill in which you make a living, also learning and refining a skill.

Pyramid or Alligator Claw: Abundance, growth, prosperity, steady income, a time of plenty

Seeker Bone or Charm: Represents the person being read.

Foot Bone: Health, Sensitivity, Awareness.

Crossroads Root: Choices, Balance, Justice, Agreements, Sacrifice

Jaw Bone: Speech, Communication or Gossip.

Teeth: Teacher or Student, Teaching or Learning

Arm Bone or Acorn: Ability to Manifest, or Endurance called for.

Coins: Wealth, Prosperity, Good Business

Owl bone or Pellet: Seeing through the darkness in any situation

Leg Bone: Support and Stability.

Snake Bone: Knowledge, Change and Renewal

Shoulder Bone: That which is being Carried.

Fox bone: Cunning is needed or Someone is deceiving you

Spirit Bone, or Bottom Spine Bone: (as it is from here that the Kundalini rises) read as Spiritual Person or Leader, a Crone or Wise Person, someone you would go to who would give you good and timely advice. Or as an awakening is in process.

Fire Bone or Metal: read as either a Red Head or a Person of Intelligence. Up it is read as Ideas, Inspiration, Illumination and Willpower. Down it represents: Forbidden Passions or Outside Influences..

Earth Bone, Emerald or Root: read as either a Brown haired or Wealthy person or, Up it reads: Business Security, Home, Family and Friends and Down; the Deception, Destruction, False people spreading false rumors.

Water Bone or Hag Stone: read as A person with Black Hair or a Creative Person; Up it is read: Compassion and Reconciliation, Healing Love, Energy into Form, Arts and Sciences. Down it represents: a hardness and unrelenting character, break up or separation, disease.

Air Bone or Feather: read as a Blond haired person, Up it is Wishes, hopes, dreams and inspiration. Down it is Conflict, or Disbursement of Energy, Chaos, the Falling apart of a Situation.

Sun Stone: Power, Energy, Life, Protection, Healing and Success. Also used as an indication of a long period of time.

Moon Stone: Secrets, Hidden Truths, a Spiritual Journey is needed to regain pieces of your lost self. Indicates a shorter period of time.

Mercury Stone: (Hematite) Strength, Victory, Balance and Wisdom. Reversed: It reflects the best and worst of yourself back at you.

Venus Stone: (Rose Quartz) It represents love in all its fashions, dignity and value. Reversed it represents emotional upset from those you care for.

Mars Stone: (Carnelian) Motivation, Leadership, Physical Power and Energy. Reversed it represents lack of motivation, being stuck, listlessness.

Jupiter Stone: (Citrine) Success, Abundance, Good Fortune and Good Luck. Reversed it means Loss, Financial Hardship, Bad Decisions, Business Failings.

Saturn Stone: (Lapis Lazuli) Truth, Intuitive Awareness, Manifestation of Desire. Reversed this stone represents a deception that you feel going on but refuse to acknowledge for fear of loss of a desire. This is actually what's holding you back from true happiness.

Uranus Stone: (Fire Opal) Spontaneous Action which bring in new Ideas, added Protection, and Money. Reversed means fear is holding you back from the change required for you to grow. Bravery is called for.

Neptune Stone: (Amethyst) Patience is called for and will lead to Prosperity. Take this time to rest and review the situation carefully. Trust your instincts.. Reversed it represents destructive compulsive behavior that will lead to ultimate loss, confusion and depression.

Pluto Stone: (Onyx) It is time to release any negative emotions, people and situations so that you may move on. Willpower and Reason are called for here so that you don't fall back into the same patterns. Reversed it says that you are hanging on to negative things because of the attention it gets you. You are afraid to lose them because you don't want to lose the attention. You are caught in a circle of your own devise that will diminish and destroy who you truly were meant to be.

In the chapter on Herbs, Roots and Woods you will find many, many more that can be used for every possible meaning. Remember, there is no set number of anything in this type of divination set. It is up to you, so you can use as many or as few as you desire.

However, it is very important that your set reflect YOU and YOUR ANCESTORS. Therefore every set and everyone's interpretation from the use of the set is completely different and unique. Since this is a method of communication between you, your ancestors and your spirits, at no time should another human ever touch it. As well, Spirits are never treated like slaves or servants, but are honored, respected and given a place of honor (like a Skull from the animal your bones came from) and proper offerings. Offerings depend on the spirit as it may be alcohol, tobacco, candy, milk and honey, dumb suppers, objects etc. Get to know your spirit and invite it along with you so you can build a friendship out of love and respect. For they can communicate with the dead, send messages to and from, and travel in places you cannot. Always remember to give offerings and alms in every situation and use them as a friend as well as a magickal partner.

Spare animal bones can be used to connect to your animal guide, they can be placed in a medicine bag or housed on your altar. Like your human spirit, the animal is free to come and go as it so chooses, but the more favorable you make its home, the more it will enjoy staying around and being your friend. They can be very useful as protectors, guides, and guardians.

Once you have gathered your collection of bones, cleaned, blessed, consecrated it and you and your ancestors have decided upon the meanings of them, then there are a few different ways in which you can throw them in which to divine the current situation at hand. You will want to make sure you also have chosen a male and female bone.

First if you have kept your bones in a fur bag, then you can open it up and use it to divine your cast on. If not you can use a separate hide, a circle on the ground, a circle on a cloth, three circle on a cloth (past , present and future), a circle divided into four quadrants, etc. There is no right or wrong way, it's whatever feels good and right to the caster. Secondly, there are a number of ways the bones can be **Cast:**

Left to Right: Past, Present and Future. Any cast outside the hide or circle are not read and have no meaning in the cast.

Out and Away: Those falling closest to you are the Past, Farthest away are future possibilities if all current roads are followed and those in the middle represent the present.

Whole Cast: The bones and curios are read as a whole interpretation of the current situation, instead of past, present and future influences.

Four Quadrants: May represent Past, Present, Future and the Unknown or Love, Money, Health and the unknown, The Seasons or the Next Four Months.

The Wheel: Divided into the twelve houses of the zodiac with each astrological house representing what they would in birth chart.

Hide Reading: Head (State of Mind), Neck (External Factors and Influences), Chest (Feelings, Heart's Desire and Motivations), Front Left Paw (Oppositions), Rear Left Paw (The Past Influences), Front Right Paw (What is needed to stay on the Right Path, also any allies or helpers will appear here), Right Rear Paw (Future Outcome), Groin (Sex, Sexuality and Patterns of Thought, Positive and Negative ones), and finally the Tail (Lessons to be Learned).

Quick Reading: Much like the Runes, the Bones can do a quick reading by pulling out three bones to represent Past, Present and Future or the First bone can represent the problem, issue or question asked. The Second bone then represents what is needed to address the problem or issue or what can be done to the result desired by the question. The Third Bone then represents the mostly likely outcome if you stay on the current path. Remember always that situations change according to the decisions of all those involved.

Patterns: Patterns in the bones may or may not be read depending on the preference of the caster. Here are some standard outlays:

Upward Triangle: Growth and Manifestation, Something coming in.

Downward Triangle: Influence or Condition is shrinking away

The I I: even lines side by side represents Harmony, Balance of Energies or two people going alongside but never connecting to each other.

The T: Blockages, One bone is blocking the other and keeping it from manifestoing (this can be good or bad)

The X : This indicates a strong Wish and the bones involved can be working with each other or against each other.

Vertical Lines: (going up and down) Represent a Yes answer, have a Male energy and bring a Dynamic outcome.

Horizontal Lines: (going left and right) Represent a No answer, have a Female energy and have a Receptive presence.

Diagonal Lines: Represent a Separation and you are to look on both sides of the lines to see what is being separated.

U or Horseshoe: Up is Good Luck (depending on your upbringing and Ancestors), and Down is bad luck or luck being poured out.

Images: In some cases the bones may suggest an Image like a car, house, human or animal. In our book The Art of Divination we have a complete Image Interpretation Guide to help you with these.

Relationships: The casting of one bone into relationship or proximity of another. This relationship can be growing or diminishing depending on the cast you use and the person being read.

Spirit Bone with the Goddess Bone: A Woman of great insight, a Mother or Helper, one who gives great advice.

Evil Eye Bone with the God Bone: Indicates the Evil Nature of Man, An Evil Man full of Jealousy, Tyranny, and possible Abuse.

Earth Bone with the Goddess Bone: Indicates a pregnancy related to the person being read or a child to come that requires the person being read to open up and receive in some way as their own.

Fire Bone with the Goddess Bone: Indicates a ether a Red Haired Woman or one with a Fiery Temper or Dominant Outgoing Personality.

Heart Bone with the God Bone: Indicates a Loving Man who is generous and giving.

Evil Eye Bone with the Pyramid: Indicates a loss of job, loss of a court case, unemployment or a hard financial situation approaching.

Evil Eye with the Earth Bone: Indicates Disease, Sickness and Ill Health, Need to change or incorporate a healthier diet.

Evil Eye with the Horseshoe: Bad Luck, Hardship, Turning of Events, Bad outcome to Court Cases.

Goddess Bone with the Air Bone: May indicate Blond Woman or one who is causing conflict.

Pyramid with the Evil Eye: Means a Business Deal or Enterprise is Delayed, Falling apart or They have gone another way.

Heart Bone with a Water Bone: A Relationship is in the Cooling Off Stage and may need to be sparked, changed or shook up.

Heart Bone with a Fire Bone: A Relationship is Heating up or becoming more passionate, or a friend will soon become a lover.

Spirt Bone with the Cross Roads Bone: The Universe has heard you and the Spirits have Granted your Wish.

Spirit Bone With Key or Heart Bone: Read UP: The Spirits are working on it and you will soon have the opportunity you desire, so open up an look for what you haven't been seeing. Or Read Down: There is a Spiritual

Reason why the path (love or money) has not opened up and this must be addressed by the seeker in some way for the situation to open up.

Again these all are simply ideas and suggestions for beginning the ground work with your own Ancestors and Spirit Guides. You must decide what works best for you and them. Consider carefully your Heritage, Culture and what you have access to, so that you have a true and deep connection to your Bones. Your Bone Set should be a very personal link connecting you to the Spirit World. Remember to always Honor them, as well as your Ancestors and Spirit Guides and you will be well rewarded!

Lucky Lithia Spell for putting up Borders

You Will Need: St. John's Wort, or St. Joan's Wort with Bay leaves, Basil, Mugwort, Cinnamon Sticks, Dried Roses, Trefoil, Vervain, and either Mint or Chia leaves. These you are to make garlands and mojos with. You will also need either black rocks or river rocks of various sizes to put down your borders with. It is always good to pile 4 or 8 together in groups or on top of each other. You will need bigger ones for outside and tiny ones to put in the corners inside. Lastly you will need green candles and gold candles.

The Spell:

Circles of green, Circles of Stone
Cinnamon and Mint and Rose all sewn
Garland within, Stones without
Protect us all around, With Luck all about!

Hung over the door, and set by the Gate
So the Blessings abound with the Fae and the Fates
A garden for the Fairy and a Home for Me
Blessed by the Wind, The Earth and the Sea!

Lord and Lady all Honor to Thee
All is now done, So Mote it Be!
(Stamp Foot!)

2 DOWSING

Dowsing consists of many things and many items can be used to get what you want from it. For this chapter we are not interested in Pendulums for Divination as that is thoroughly discussed in our The Art of Divination book. We are here to take it a step further and practice the use of Pendulums, Plum Bobs, and Rods for the art of finding things. Dowsing rods can be a Y shaped stick made of usually made of Witch Hazel, Willow, a Peach Tree or a green branch found on the property. L shaped copper rods with or without and insert chamber for the desired material can be used as well as a Pendulum or Plumb bob. At times a mosaic Rod or Rod of Aaron has been held up in the air and asked a yes or no question to ascertain the presence of the sought after substance (if the rod moves it is a yes, no movement indicates a no.).

Dowsing (Doodle bugging, Water Witching) has been used for centuries to find hidden water wells, underground streams, oil reserves, caves, buried metals and ores, gravesites, minerals and gemstones, sex determination of eggs, diagnosing car problems, diagnosing health issues, locating fish, sport hunting, and more recently to find lost septic tanks, utility lines, leech fields, water and gas pipelines, people, murder weapons, pets, ley lines and lines of geopathic stress. Actually dowsing can be used for finding anything from the fidelity of a lover to victims of an avalanche, the uses are only limited to your imagination.

A pendulum may be moved over a map to cut down the area or an L rod may be used to find a direction to go. Y shaped branches will begin a downward pull when the substance is found, and the L rods will make an X if one is held in each hand.

Having an Insert or a piece of what you are looking for on hand is very helpful as well as Visualizing what you are looking for and keeping it in the forefront of your mind as false images can emerge for one who isn't practiced with the skill. As with say, Gold, there may be many different elements that contain particles of it like pyrite or marcasite so it's important to clearly define that which you desire in your mind's eye.

There are four different types of dowsing as defined by the American Society of Dowers. (1) Field Dowsing: the use of dowsing which involves locating water, objects, and so forth on a given terrain. This is called Witching the area; (2) Map Dowsing: the dowser locates the target using a map or sketch, often accompanied by the use of a pendulum. There are no distance limits here, since the dowser can locate their target even 10,000 miles away; (3) Remote Dowsing: Witching the area is not required in this approach, instead the use of Astral Projection is used to locate the target from a distance of up to several miles or continents away. The Army has done experiments with this kind to obtain information and locate people which brings us to our last method; (4) Information Dowsing: the dowser obtains needed information on any subject with neither space nor time limits. Information dowsing not only saves time, but can be a great aid to increase the scope of the dowsing process.

However, please note that the very experienced dowser can use any instrument, or none but their own being. It's simply a matter of getting your muscle memory to develop and practice, practice, practice. One way to practice is by using bottles filled with different elements that are put behind a block out label (a label you can't see through) so you can't see the contents in the bottle. Or have someone hide the bottles and you seek the one you are looking for by divining around the house. Or go outside in your yard and walk around. If you don't find any sources, then stretch out the garden hose and turn it on. The water creates a pattern of energy that you should immediately feel with either a Y rod or L rods. Even after you turn the water off and roll up the hose there will still for a time be left a ghost presence of this energy. Remember dowsing requires you not only feeling the energy but communicating with it, asking it questions, receiving answers, opening yourself up to the Universal Energies.

Another way to practice is upon the Human Aura. Start with your rods crossed next to someone heart and slowly walk backwards. The rods will begin moving outwards and will become straight out as soon as you reach the outside of their Aura. Now ask them to think of things they Love and measure how this expands the Aura. Then ask them to think of things that make them Angry and measure how their Aura shrinks inside them.

A Third way to practice is with the Geopathic Stress lines upon your own property. Geopathic Stress can cause illness, the feeling of being drained, unmotivated, and health problems of all kinds. This may be due to underground water paths, emotional imprints, a spiritual presence, an electrical or magnetic charge going through the area.

Start by doing a perimeter around the building. Anytime the rods cross instead of stay forward, mark the spot. Then go inside and do the same. The lines should then link up and be clearly seen. The Farm House that I rented when I first came to North Carolina was beside a river with a connection to it beside the house. It was also over 100 years old and had a septic tank. The initial energies drove my daughter and I to anger and tears for no reason and so after careful divining I placed foot long copper rods in a number of areas, including windows and doorways and everything was at once, exceedingly better.

You may of course divine that it is a piece of furniture that causes a discomfort in a room as it may have been with a negative or abusive person or been the place where a very ill person always sat. If that is the case, then search the further chapters on how to clean the furniture with a proper wash. Include a drumming away of the spiritual element as well as finishing up with a proper floral essence like a good Florida water (my own recipe for Florida Water is all the left over drops from all the essences I have used in my own spiritual concoctions).

If it is a Spirit and you aren't familiar with how to work with spirits then please get someone who is. If you are capable of traversing a spirit then please do so, by listening to it and then helping it onward. Use your intuition. Hone it. Go on walkabouts and practice talking to not only Spirit but the Spirit within us all.

Next try Archeological or Sacred Sites and practice dowsing there. Examples (depending on where you live) may be Indian Mounds, Standing Stones, Old Churches and Graveyards etc. as may sites were just naturally buildt along ley lines and natural currents. These currents may even present as spirals. It is best when practicing to go out when as few people as possible are present so that you can keep your concentration (but refrain from going out alone as the buddy system has saved many lives!). You will also notice that when dowsing with a partner that the two of you will pick up on different energies. This is completely normal as we all, each and every one of us, have our own unique vibrational frequency and this effects how the earth's frequencies and vibrations relate to us. Don't be swayed, Physical Dowsing (Water, Metals, Oil etc.) is completely different than energy dowsing. For one thing you can't hold it in your hand and everybody's visualization of it is distinct and different. However, working with these energies will helping you hone your physical dowsing skills as it will make you awaken and feel the energies.

Practice helps you establish pathways of memory for your intellect and intuition to find common ground. Much like getting a good or a bad feeling when you meet someone, you need to establish a connection for you to rely on. Instinct can sometimes seem easier for a fish seeking food, or a dog when it first meets a stranger, but we are all part of this same energy and are reflectors of it just the same. There is a collective consciousness, a force or energy field around all things, it's just opening up to the reality of it. Soon even your muscles will react to different levels in energy as you come across them and they will build a memory of how it feels.

Dowsing through Remote Viewing begins as a form of Telepathy. You at any time of the day or night are either projecting or receiving energy, thoughts, information etc. This can be seen easily in your everyday life. For instance have you ever thought of an invention only to see its reality six months later? That energy you projected was broadcast into the Universe then picked up by someone who was receiving. You didn't have to do anything but think it, and it came to be. Remote Viewing is very much the same thing. Only this time you desire to receive and so you must get into a place of not thinking yet feeling with your being. Put up your borders or do your circle. Then go for a walk in your mind. Observe everything. Start with a place you often go, see every flower, plant and tree. Talk to the birds and the animals. Start by locating a favorite thing. Remember it and then do the same walk in the physical world.

If you have a Dowsing Partner then work together in separate locations. One of you set up to project and the other to receive. Keep it simple, it will grow. For instance one day when picking up my son from middle school, my daughter Cat decided to sit in the front seat. I reminded her that her brother was going to toss her in the back. She looked at me and said, not today. Today I say he will get in the back and want to be there. That is exactly what happened. She projected a thought, he received it and acted accordingly. I explained to her it's not proper to control peoples actions with our very thoughts, but I admire her pluck, and it is good to project ahead of say a Business Meeting or Interview to get appropriate results. However, again, practice makes perfect, so start with projecting a parking space when you go shopping. See it in your mind's eye and have it open up for you just as you get there (I do this one a lot!). Be careful of what you project though, as I once projected an aura of invisibility around myself so sound that the neighbors asked my son where I had been for the past two months and my vehicle got hit twice (and myself almost three times!).

Now information dowsing requires that you project and receive at the same time. There are three types. One involves dowsing a person or animal (while you are standing over them) for the purposes of healing (spiritual, emotional or physical) and receiving the information necessary as to the affected part or what to do to heal it. This is first accomplished by the use of a pendulum or your hands, to find the affected part and then asking questions with your mind as to what herb and how much of it to use in the cure or filling yourself with healing energy and projecting it into them. You could even put the Medicine Woman healing techniques in this category as the Medicine Man goes into the other world to ascertain the problem and find a cure for it. The Medicine Woman may either then provide the necessary cure or cure the patient themselves by projecting the necessary energy into the affected part.

In the second way you are projecting your spirit or astral self to a place where you can gather information while remaining relaxed and aware. This can be as simple as going to seek the answers on tomorrow's test to visiting the Library of Alexandria or Traveling to another Planet or Dimension. This form is often used to access the Akashic Records, much like a Shaman's Journey into one's self. The most important thing to remember about this is that you must feel safe while doing it. So setting up your borders and your circle is doubly important. As well, you must stay receptive and open to the information you find. This isn't always easy. Some things we don't want to know, even about ourselves. Sometimes ignorance is bliss. But Knowledge is Spiritual Growth, and to refuse to grow is to die.

Thirdly involves remote healing. This requires you to project your energy at a specified target, gather information, and send healing to the affected area. Reiki Masters do this repeatedly. Sometimes one healing session isn't enough, sometimes it is. In the system of Reiki, certain symbols are used to meditate on and project which mean healing and travel. Much like the Medicine Man working on a client from a distance, a Reiki Master sends out and receives knowledge and then sends out healing. Any person can master this through their own technique if given enough practice and time. I have a friend of mine, Paul Harry Simons, who lives in Brazil, who will decide to call me upon the odd occasion I am not feeling well and then heal me remotely. He is neither a Reiki Master or a Shaman, but he is a Wondrous Healer. He has honed his art and can now receive my outgoing signal for help and project the healing back to me when I am too scattered to do it myself! I in turn do the same back for him. It is important in the Universe, even for a solitary, to accept the people set in your path. You have no idea how wonderfully important they will become!

3 EGGS & COCONUTS

Besides making cascarilla powder, eggs have long been used in divination and the breaking of curses. Due to their molecular structure the closely resemble our own structure. When Rolling the Egg, the molecular structure of the egg white will become affected. If the person is cursed or hexed, there will be a color change, an off smell or a mar in the structure of the egg (blood, clots, figures etc.). This will indicate the need to repeat until the egg white becomes clear, and thereby the presence of the curse is considered gone. A coconut has the same properties with the milk in the center. While not always used on the human body, it is better used on a home or property as it can stand up to being rolled all around it better. Here are some ways to use them:

To Read Someone with an Egg:
Pass the egg over the body by gently rolling it from the top of the body to the waist. Then do the arms, shoulders and fingers, across and behind the abdomen and down each leg including the toes and heels. The egg is then kept under the bed of the person, or upon their mantel or an altar until the next day, then put into a bowl half filled with water to examine it.

To Rid Yourself of a Curse:
You must purchase a brown fresh egg before noon of that day. Make sure that you start this when the moon is waning. It is very important that this egg be fresh. Place this egg in a brown bag and tie the neck of the bag with a black cloth string. Place this bag under your bed. Each night before going to bed, you must open this bag and take the egg out and rub it all over your body. When done, put the egg back into the bag, take a deep breath and blow three times into the bag.

When you are blowing into the bag, you must imagine that all the bad luck is leaving your body, via your breath. When done, place the bag back under your bed. Do this for nine days. At the end of nine days, take the bag with the egg and dispose of it outside your home (to a place that you would not normally pass by). Bury it, walk backwards away from it 3 steps from it, throw salt, turn around and don't look back!.

Note: Each time that you blow into the bag, you must immediately tie it back up. If by the end of seven days you notice that your bag is moving on its own. Stop, and dispose of the bag immediately. **Never Look in the Bag!** Make sure that the bag is secure. We are not responsible for any misuse, or actions that may results from the use of this powerful spell. Do not play with this. Only do this if you are serious about destroying the bad luck in your life.

Nordic Egg Reading:
After passing it over the body, the egg is pierced at both ends and the white is blown out into a bowl half filled with water. This bowl is then set inside the bedroom, or upon a hearth and the images are examined the next day for the images they make or hold.

To Cleanse Someone:
Pass the egg over the entire body and break it. If it the egg is marred in anyway then keep repeating until a clean egg is broken

NOTES: never put an egg down the drain if it goes to a septic tank ! I can't believe the amount of people who don't understand not to do this! The curse remains on your property. Only put it down the sink or drain if it goes down to a sewer or run off. Unless of course you want it back!

Ostara Fertility Spell:
For this talisman you will need a small green circle of cloth, a needle and thread, a piece of paper with a picture of you and your mate, eggshells, and some fertility herbs such as bistort, carrot (root and tail), nuts of all kinds, wheat, myrtle, rice, rye, barley, pine cones, dried corn or popcorn, acorns, juniper, pine, cedar, lemongrass, honeysuckle, and turnips (use only what you have, all are not necessary to have for the spell to work). You may also include stones associated with fertility such as holey stones, stones with two points side by side, or geodes. Handle all of the ingredients, infusing them with your desire to have a baby. Then place them together in the green cloth and sew them shut. Holding the talisman between your hands and your belly, say **The Spell:** Charm of egg and life to be, power of fertility, come to me. Like the Goddess Ostara, whose blood mingles with mine, so shall I give birth in nine months' time.

Leave the charm under your mattress while having sex during your fertile time with your partner. Then wear the talisman like a mojo bag or a necklace over your belly, renewing your intent by chanting the above quatrain when you can, to assist you in becoming pregnant.

To Make Someone Move, Go Away or Leave You Alone:
Inscribe their name on a black candle. Dress the candle with oil and roll in black and red pepper. For three nights burn the candle with a paper request for this person to go away while repeating the spell 13 times. **The Spell:** Loki, Rabbit, Crow, take them far from this place that we know, bit by bit, let them go, far from here, Loki, Rabbit, Crow!. Then take the ashes (from the paper burnings) and some bloodroot with graveyard dust from 9 soldiers (or officers of the law) and seal it into a black mojo bag. Make 4 of these. At 4 am take one and bury under or by their front steps, throw one upon their roof, tuck one under their bumper or tire of their vehicle (or bury in the graveyard), and then burn one with your request that they leave, scattering the ashes to the four directions.

To do Harm to a Person:
You must obtain a worn piece of clothing like a sock, or a shirt or apron with pockets. Put graveyard dirt and three sewing needles wrapped in black thread inside it with either nine rose thorns stuck in a chicken heart or nine black chicken feathers. Write the person's name on the item 13 times or write it on a piece of paper 13 times with any other information like their birthdate or address with it. Either bury it by a place they pass by, or at a crossroads or a graveyard at 4am or 4pm saying: **The Spell:** Morrigan, Morrigan, Great Washer at the Ford, Blood and Doom, Blood and Doom, Be not ignored! Take (name) away with you, to where the blood is poured, Seal their doom, Great Morrigan and add them to your hoard!

Egg Spell for Returning the Evil Sent to you Back to the Sender:
Obtain a new white egg. Put all your identifying information on it (name, birthdate, numbers, fingerprints, anything that identifies you as you). Raise your energy and place it into the egg saying 13 times **The Spell:** Blackbird, Raven, Crow; This person who hexes I do not know, but inside this egg a bird be, flap and coo as if you are me. Crow, Blackbird, Raven, in this way you will defend, playing the injured, whilst flying it back to them! Now bury the egg or put it in a tree or place it near to who you think your enemy may well be!

To Return a Solider to You:
Get 3 fresh eggs, salt and a piece of clothing that belongs to your solider. Write any information you can on the piece of clothing including their name, rank, battalion etc. Write a heartfelt letter to Freya to asking for the return of your soldier. Then carefully wrap the letter, the three eggs and salt up in the clothing and go to a place where two roads make one. Bury this bundle saying 13x **The Spell:** Freya, dear Freya, let not my solider be taken to Folkvangr or Valhalla. Let them be brave in the battles they must endure.

But when they are through, bring them back here! Keep them complete, safe and sound, until in my arms, they are once more bound!

Egg Spell for a Wish:
Write your wish on a post it note, rolling it up tightly afterwards. This should be very small. Next decorate the egg with colors and symbols regarding your wish, Then take a pin and make a small hole in both ends and blow out the egg, replacing it with the tiny rolled up post it inside. Hold the Egg and say **The Spell:** Ostara, Ostara, Eostre! Be it Far or Be it Near, Bring my Wish to me Right Here! 13x Now either place it on your Altar or bury it near your front steps.

Egg Bath to Banish Negativity:
In a piece of cheesecloth, put an whole egg, salt, Mugwort, Rosemary, Bay Laurel Leaves, Basil, Fennel Seeds, Anise and a cut Lime. Float these in a Warm Bath while lighting a Red Candle and Chanting **The Spell:** Cailleach, Cailleach, Blessed destroyer and Fate, Take all Evil and Negativity from me, and lock it in behind your gate! Post Dormarth to guard it there, so never will it come back here! (Bury when finished)

Egg Spell for a Soul Mate to Appear to you:
On the New Moon, Take a red cloth, Two Eggs, Angelica Root and Orris Root, Red String, Rose Petals, 13 Balm of Gilead Buds, Lavender, and Elecampane. Write down EXACTLY what you desire in a Mate (be as exact as possible including any physical attributes desired, but leave a little wiggle room for what you are willing to accept as well). Burn a Red candle and chant or sing 13x times towards all the ingredients upon the red cloth **The Spell:** Branwen, Freyja, Aine, Bring two halves and make them whole again! I search for my Soul Mate and They search for me, Bring them here upon my doorstep, so our love can now be! Now wrap it all up, tie it with the read string and bury it beside your door step.

Egg Spell for Prosperity:
Break an egg in half saying **The Spell:** Manannan Mac Lir and Freyr, Bring Prosperity here, My finances though broke they be, can grow like flowers underneath the great oak tree! (13X) Now fill the egg halves with flower seeds, hold the two halves together and plant them under the oak tree nearest to your home.

NOTE: A Coconut can be used like an egg in most spells as it is a container with a watery insides.

Using a Coconut to rid a House of Past Evils:

A coconut can be more easily rolled around a house with a broom without breaking than an egg. Do this before moving into a new place with a new broom and be sure to get inside all the closets and to reach, if you can, all levels of your new place. Sing or Chant **The Spell:** Frigg, Hestia, Brigid, as around I move this grid, find all evil that is hid, in every corner, under every lid, and by this coconut, this house now rid!

A Coconut Spell for Driving a Person Crazy:

Light a black candle. Open up one of the holes in the coconut but be careful to not pour any of the milk out. Write the name of the person and any identifying information about them on a piece of paper. Use the paper live a funnel and add mandrake powder or Datura root powder and Morning Glory Seeds to the inside of the coconut (you can add other herbal hallucinogens you desire as well) and then wind up the paper tight and place it inside the coconut as well. Seal it well with the black wax. Now pick it up and chant your intentions into it ; **The Spell:** Arawan, Hel, Persephone, make (name) as crazy as can be, Thoughts askew, not able to rest, Brain so jumbled, a total mess, unable to function or think completely, so all around will now see, (name's) as crazy as can be, Arawan, Hel, Persephone! Now either bury it on their property or where they will pass by or toss it in moving water like a river or the sea to take them far away.

Coconut Spell to Destroy an Enemy:

Light a black candle. Open up one of the holes of the coconut, being careful not to spill any of its milk. Write the name of your enemy on a piece of paper and cross it out in black ink nine times. Write any other identifying information of your enemy on the back of the paper. Roll it into a funnel and put in tobacco, belladonna, oleander or foxglove, and either mistletoe or cocklebur ground up inside. Insert the paper and seal with the black wax. Now pick it up and chant or sing your intentions into it; **The Spell:** Hecate, Hecate, Goddess of the Crossroads, Steal (name) from their comfy abode. Hecate, Hecate, Keeper of the Keys, Lock up (Name) and do with them as you please! Hecate, Hecate, Beautiful Goddess revered, now take (name) far away from here!

Coconut Spell to rid Yourself of a Curse:

Roll the coconut over yourself, back and front, head to foot, at least three times saying **The Spell:** Lucifer, Lucifer of the Green and Grey, Take all Evil from me Away! 13X. Make sure you take the coconut to a place where one road ends into another and bury it there.

4 SALTS & BATHS

Salts are used in Circle Casting, Divination and Protection, where a Bath is used for Purification before doing spell work or for Cleansing after spell work is done so that no spirits stick to thee. Here are some classic recipes:

White Salt: can be table salt, rock salt, ice cream salt, or Epsom salt. Used for baths or circles, for protection, for removing stuck on evil, or for use in cleansing or circle salt.

Red Salt: white salt mixed with red brick dust or red ochre. Used to banish evil or for protection.

Black Salt: otherwise called Witch's Salt is the ashes from all the spells you have worked mixed with a protective oil and white salt. It is used as extra protection when dong baneful magick.

Grey Salt: Salt that has been used on a road, presumably near an enemies or intended victims home. Used as part of a tag lock or homing device for a spell.

Reversal Salt: a mix of white, black, and red salt with ground crab legs and cascarilla powder. Used for reversing spells or making evil lose its tracks, therefore being unable to find you.

Summoning Salt: a mixture of salt, graveyard dirt, and sulfur, saltpeter or sugar. Used to summon the spirits of the dead. Take great care against possession, and use a Rowan staff to send them back right after.

Cleansing Salt: white salt with rosemary, bay leaves, and sage. Can be kept in a bowl and used to cleanse crystals or anything else that may have picked up bad vibrations before you bought it.

Prosperity Salt: white salt with allspice, nutmeg, Palm Rosa grass or vetiver and cinnamon. Used for a circle salt when doing prosperity magick or to carry in a mojo or put in a cash register in your desk at work.

Love Salt: white salt, elecampane, jasmine, orange peel, and vanilla. Used as a summoning salt in Love Spells to bring lovers together or to gain a love.

Salt Bath: to make a salt bath, you will make a batch of salt, baking soda and herbs to keep in a jar. Then remove as needed into a cheese cloth that is tied with string and floated in the tub with you or used in the shower as you would a washcloth scrubbing yourself from top to bottom. If you are lacking a herb, then an odd number of drops of essential oils will suffice.

Coventina's Purification Bath: Mugwort, Peppermint and Eucalyptus with salt, and dry milk. For use before doing spells or on the new and full moons. **The Spell:** Coventina, Celtic Goddess of the waters, purify me. Open up my pores and help me to see. Make my words brave and true, in all the spells I am about to do!

Aeron's Purification Bath: Frankincense, Mint and Rosemary with dry milk, and salt. For use before doing rituals and on Sabbaths. **The Spell:** Aeron, purify my body, soul and mind, as I lay in your arms and unwind, Wrap me with in your sunshine, and warm me with your words so kind. As I lay in this water here, may you whisper in my ear, so I give homage true, to the Gods and Goddesses of this Sabbath, as is their just due!

Artemis's Purification Bath: Allspice, Vanilla, and Juniper with salt, dry milk and honey. For use before doing spells and rituals on the equinoxes and solstices. **The Spell:** O Artemis, dear maiden divine, cleanse and purify this heart of mine. For upon the cross hairs of the earth, Let my magick come forth and give birth. Make my spells aim, just and true, just like your arrows dear Artemis, may justice come due!

Bel's Cleansing Bath: Sage, Rosemary and Lavender with salt and baking soda. For use after doing spells to cleanse yourself of any remaining aspects. It is best when doing a cleansing bath to sing nonsense songs to confuse any spirits. **The Song:** Mairzy doats and dozy doats ad liddle lamzy divey, a kiddley divey too, wooden shoe. And if the words sound queer and funny to your ear, a little bit jumbling jivey, then sing mares eat oats and does eat oats and little lambs eat ivy!

Frigg's Cleansing Bath: Rosemary, Rue and Angelica with salt and baking soda. For use after visiting graveyards and crossroads. It is best when doing a cleansing bath to sing nonsense songs to confuse the spirits. **The Song:** Oh, I was born one night one morn, when the whistle went toot, toot (TOOT, TOOT!) you can bake a steak or fry a cake when the mud pies are in bloom does 6 and 6 make 9? does ice grow on a vine? is old man Joe an eskimo in the good ol' summertime? Oh, a loop-de-loop in the noodle soup, go give socks a shine. I'm guilty judge, I stole the fudge 3 cheers for auld Lang sine! I cannot tell a lie, I hooked an apple pie, it's on a tree, beneath the sea, above the bright blue sky! Oh, Easter eggs don't shave their legs, their children will have ducks (QUACK, QUACK!) I'd rather buy a lemon pie for 47 bucks way down in Barcelona, I jumped into a foamea, but that is all balonea, Patterisky blow your horn, TOOT, TOOT!

Lugh's Cleansing Bath: Dragons Blood, Frankincense and Juniper with salt and baking soda, For use after doing Baneful magick. It is best when doing a cleansing bath to then sing nonsense songs after to confuse the spirits. **The Songs:** Great green globs of greasy grimy gopher guts, Mutilated monkey meat, little birdies dirty feet, and all those things that I really, really like to eat, And I forgot my spoon! – This is the song that never ends, it goes on and on my friends, some people started singing it not knowing what it was, and they just kept on singing it forever just because…(song repeats)

Lakshmi's Prosperity Bath: Pumpkin pie spice, with Basil and Orange with salt and baking soda. Used for bringing unexpected luck and money to a person. **The Spell:** Lakshmi, Lakshmi, Lakshmi, Goddess of Wealth and Prosperity, one this day draw money to me, draw money to me; Shreem Brzee OM Brzee Namaha! (the last bit should be drawn out to vibration and said 108 times!)

The Fate's Wealth Bath: Palm Rosa oil, vetiver, lemon grass, citronella, and ginger with salt and honey. Used to bring wealth and prosperity to all business prospects or to gain employment. **The Spell:** Cernunnos, Teutates, Odin, Tara, bring wealth to me from near and far! Tara, Cernunnos, Teutates, Odin; bring wealth to me from out and from within! Odin, Tara, Cernunnos, Teutates; bring wealth to me from the Fates!

Love Come to Me Bath: Elecampane, Honeysuckle, and Jasmine with Salt, Milk and Honey. Used to attract and bind love to you. **The Spell:** Clidha, Frigg, Sjofn, Aine; bring love to me by your hand, across the seas and across the sand, across the hills in every land, Clidha, Frigg, Sjofn, Aine; make them mine as fast as you can!

Come Hither Bath: Vanilla, High John, Success oil with Benzoin, Salt and Baking Soda. To summon a lusty love or opportunities of such. **The Spell:** Herne, Cernunnos, Lofn, Pan; put upon me your magick hand, fill me with the essence of, sexy lusty passionate love! Feel my senses, light my eyes, draw to me, girls and guys! Let me have my pick and then, send me out to conquer again!

Four for Abundance Bath: Mint, Dill, Blackberry leaves, Dandelion and Violet in a bath with Milk and Honey. **The Spell:** Copia, Abundantia, Fortuna, Sors; open wide all the doors, unlock them all with your keys, and make me as abundant as can be! In this land of milk and honey, supply me avenues, all filled with money! Each and Every way I turn, let fortune come and a living earn!

Three for Good Health: Peppermint, Thyme, Kava Root, and Peony with Epsom salt. **The Spell:** Airmed, Sirona, Eir; Heal me as I lay bare, from my feet to my hair, and everything between there! Airmed, Sirona, Eir!

None Can Compare Beauty Bath: Oats, Chamomile, Bay Leaves, Gotu Kola and Calendula. **The Spell:** Epona, Venus, Aphrodite, make me comely, make me lovely! A beauty rare, none can compare, so all who see me, will also love me!

Dian Cecht Aches Away Bath: Clove, Lavender, Peppermint, Witch Hazel, and Meadowsweet. **The Spell:** Dian Cecht take away my pain, so I can move and live again! Dian Cecht come to me and take, every single little ache! Dian Cecht set me free, of all the pain that now plagues me!

Lilith's Bewitching: Jezebel Root, Orris Root, Calamus Root, Vanilla Bean, and Civet Oil, with Salt, Dry Milk and Honey. **The Spell:** Lilith, Dark Goddess of the Night; Increase My Powers, Give them Flight, Raise Me up to new Heights, and to All who fall within my sight, let them be Bewitched by Me this night!

Persephone's Love: Spikenard, Frankincense, Sandalwood, Lotus, and Honeysuckle, with Salt. **The Spell:** Persephone, Queen of Shades; upon this water where I bathe, from me now do create, a perfect loving supportive mate! Bring their image to me now, lock it in my mind somehow, so when I then see them true, our love will be bound and stick like glue!

Ganesh's Treasure: Bergamot, Cypress, Five Finger Grass, Licorice root, Nutmeg with Epsom Salt. **The Spell Mantra:** Lord Ganesh's Treasure come to Me: Om Gam Ganapataye Namaha Om Saubhagya-vardhanaahya Namaha! (18 times for 10 days drawing out the sounds into a sing chant)

Vishnu's Preserver: Rue, Cinnamon, Linden Flower, Hollyhock, and Pineapple in Epsom salt. **The Spell Mantra:** Lord Vishnu, Preserver and Multiplier, Come to Me: Namo Bhagavate Vasudevaya, Om Shreem krishnaya Shreem, Shreem Shreem govindaya gopalaya goloka, sundaraya sathyaya nithyaya paramathmane paraya, vykhanasaya vyrajamoorthaye, meghathmane Shreem narasimhavapushe namah! (18X for 10 days drawing out the letter sounds into a sing chant)

Goddess Clarity Bath: Dandelion, Basil, Fenugreek, Pine, Heather, Mugwort, and Myrrh with salt. **The Spell:** Holy Goddess most divine, clear all thoughts from my mind, let me relax in this bath right here, so you can give me answers, soft and clear!

The Oracle at Delphi: Anise, Jasmine, Honeysuckle, Mugwort, Lemon Grass, and Mace with salt and baking soda. **The Spell:** Oracle of Delphi, Navel of the Earth, raise upon these waters vapors, visions of great worth! Open up my mind's eye, so that it can see, all the answers that I seek, in revealing prophesy!

Black Cat Bath: High John Root, Five Finger Grass, Wisdom Root, Mandrake, and Peach oil in salt and dried milk. **The Spell:** Black cat, cross my path, good fortune bring to hearth and home, and when I'm away, bring me luck, wherever that I choose to roam! (13X)

Fiery Passions of Love: Damiana, Patchouli OR Musk, Orris Root, Vanilla and Lotus oil in salt. **The Spell:** Fiery Passions build between you and me, Fiery Passions that won't let us be, Fiery Passions between you and I, Fiery Passions that light up the Night! (7X)

Be True to Me: Lavender, Rose Petals, Angelica Root, Orris Root and Sandalwood with salt. **The Spell:** Be True to Me, both day and night, Be true to me, even when we fight; Be true to me, both night and day, Be true to me and never stray! (9X)

Setting up the Wards: Clover, Coconut, Begonia, Chrysanthemum and Clove in Salt. **The Spell:** I set up the wards in north and south, I set up the wards around this house, I set up the wards in east and west, I set them up against every test; I strengthen the wards in south and north, no evil can ever step on my porch, I strengthen the wards in west and east, strong they are against every beast! I set up the wards of high and low, strong they are against every foe, I strengthen the wards of low and high, now no evil can ever get by! (13X)

5 POWDERS & MINERALS

Banishing Powder: Coffee, Chili Pepper, Astragals, Cumin and Myrrh. Used for banishing lower spirits and evil forces. **The Spell:** Aife, Aife, Warrior Goddess who gave us the magick alphabet of the deities, come to my aid now and hear me, banish these spirits from this space, put them all back into their place, clear them out and leave no trace! Aife, Aife, Aife! (stomp your foot on the last three, and holler her name with great authority!)

Bend Over Powder: Licorice Root powder, Rose, Frankincense and Honeysuckle powders. Used as a controlling powder for a number of reasons, like keeping someone working at a job instead of quitting and leaving you with all the bills, having an ex send you your child support, making sure the pedophile down the street is never home, etc. **The Spell:** Red Rover, Red Rover, bend (name) on over! Bend (name) to my desire, Bend (name) to my will; Bend (name) to do whatever I need of their skill!

Bygul and Trigul or Black Cat Powder: Black Cat Hair (naturally shed by petting), Tobacco (natural tobacco is always used unless poisoning someone, there are several Native American brands that are straight tobacco), Lucky Hand Root, High John Root powder and Honeysuckle Vine. Used by gamblers to bind luck to their hands in games of chance. **The Spell:** Freyja your cats, lend me this day, for lucky I'll be, and always stay!

Black Pepper Powder: Just what it says. Black pepper powder is used for protection from evil and for driving people away, like in Hot Foot Powder. Some Black Pepper Berries kept in the corners of your house are a nice easy ward to keep out all kinds of evil. **The Spell:** Black pepper, black pepper, evening accord, Keep evil at bay upon my word! (now make the sign of the pentacle wheresoever you place it).

Brick Dust: This is just as it sounds, it is the dust from fired red clay brick. In order to make brick from clay one must be cured in a kiln under 1800 degrees for 7 days or at the very least been in a house fire. Without this curing in the fire the brick is not suited for magick as the iron oxide contained within have long been known to repel negative energy and entities. Bricks from places where someone would do magick are of course best as are bricks from a holy place like a monastery. But as long as it is a natural clay brick and not one made of concrete and you have permission from the spirits then you can gain one from old crumbling homes, roads or build sites. Never gather from a Mental Institution or a Prison. Evil cannot step over the line of dust, therefore thieves are kept at bay. Red brick dust is associated with strength and strong walls and therefore is used for warding and make great borders. Cleansing in spring water or smudging with Sage or Frankincense, is always a good practice. Grind in a counter clockwise manner to banish negativity or send things away (clockwise to bring things in) and call on your Gods and Goddesses while doing so. Red Ochre clay dust can also be used and is very effective magickally and medicinally. Ground hematite, red iron ox Adding brick dust to chamber lye (urine) or vinegar is called reddening (this is added like bluing is to a wash) for protection and used around or in vehicles, person, home. Iron oxide powder, Osun powder, menstrual blood and red henna powder substitutes in a pinch. Also used in Protective mojo bags , poppets and border bottles, and put on top of cursed objects to nullify them. **The Spell:** Grind and grind and grind away, keep all evil that comes at bay, banish all evil from my sight, send it far off into the night!

Cascarilla Powder: This is a chalk made from the eggshells of black chickens. Black chickens hold a special curing power in all religions and regions across the world where their black meat is considered to have special healing properties. As well they have long been known to keep evil and curses at bay. Black Chicken Breeds are: Black Autralorp, Black Silkies, Ayam Cemani, Svart Hona, Korean Ogol, Yeonsan Ogye, Kadaknath, Sumatra, Jersey Giant, Castilian Black, Cubalaya, Black Cochin, Langshan, Black Orpington, Breda, La Fleche, Minorca, Transylvanian Naked Neck, Utrerana Negra, Crevecoeur, and Andalusian Blue may be considered. Used for purification and protection as well as cleansing, making sigils and magick markings on a table or ground, summoning, repelling negative energy, guarding from evil, malicious magick or disease, and magick rituals. Can also be added to any bath or wash for added protection. **The Spell:** Pound and grind and pound some more, let no evil pass through my door, let no evil in my circle tread, in my house or in my head, let no evil see or hear me, and close their mouths so they can't mirror me!

Cerridwen's Powder: Made with Red brisk dust, Cascarilla powder, set with 9 iron nails, Linden flower, Amaranth, Sea salt, and Sulphur powders. Add yourself some Rowan root and Bay leaves for protection and always be polite and honor the spirits you summon with a small offering before and a large one just as you send them back. NEVER leave a spirit wandering about! (however if you do get in trouble, our The Art of the Boogity book has some tricks on "how to make it better" for you!). **The Spell:** Cerridwen, Cerridwen, I call to summon thee; to look in your cauldron for images of prophesy! Cerridwen, Cerridwen, interpret now for me, all the images that you therein now see. Cerridwen, Cerridwen, grant to me the key, let the knowledge pass now, of the images unto me!

Crown of Success Powder: Five finger Grass, High John, Low John and Dixie John powders with Linden Flowers. Used to bring success to any situation or in any spell. **The Spell:** Rosemerta, Rosemerta, Crown of Success, come to me now and triple bless! Rosemerta, Rosemerta, Cornucopia of the land, come to me now and put success in my hand!

Hekate's Crossing Powder: Devil's Shoestring Root, Cayenne pepper, Vetiver, Crossroads dirt, crushed insects and Gum Arabic. Used for crossing or cursing someone, like a murderer, rapist or pedophile, or someone who has injured or harmed you in some way. A good way to cross someone is to put it where they will walk over it or put it under their desk or on their car door handle, etc. **The Spell:** Hekate, Hekate, Crossroads Queen; cross poor (name) to sight's unseen! Hekate, Hekate, Mistress of the Craft, banish poor (name) far from my path! Hekate, Hekate, Sorceress Divine, take poor (name) down to hell and bind!

Court Case Powder: Marjoram, Tobacco, Low John, Honeysuckle, Irish Moss. To gain the upper hand in a court case when a judgement has been made against you, or to lower a sentence and gain the judge's mercy. **The Spell:** John, John go ahead of me, put mercy in the heart of all that I see. John, John, hear my words true, bring mercy upon all that I do! John, John, I know you are near, put mercy in the ears of all that can hear!

Commanding Powder: Bitter Root, Poppy and Mullein. When it is necessary to take command of a situation like if your partner has a gambling habit and you need to control the money so they won't lose it all. **The Spell:** Daghdha, Daghdha, All Father of the Tuatha De Danann; put dear (name) under my command! Put dear (name) under my rule, no longer able to act the fool! Put dear (name) under my subjection, for we know it's for their own protection!

Compelling Powder: Datura Root Powder, Mandrake Powder and Poppy Powder. Used when you need to compel someone to give you your just payment or due. Works exceedingly well if they are somehow made to breathe it in. **The Spell:** Aphrodite, Aphrodite, all fall under your spell, when you wear your magick girdle, each one is compelled! Aphrodite, Aphrodite, go now in front of me, wear your magick girdle for only (name) to see! Aphrodite, Aphrodite, work your magick rite, and make them pay me back, within a fortnight!

Confusion Powder: Poppy oil, Quassia Root, Black Mustard Seed and Couch Grass powders. Used to confuse an enemy or spirits and put them under your control. **The Spell:** Eris, Goddess of chaos, strife and discord; come into (name's) life and be not ignored! Eris, goddess of discord, chaos and strife, confuse, mess up and control (name's) life! Eris, goddess of strife, discord and chaos, see that (name) suffers immeasurable loss!

Hel's Damnation Powder: Sweet Flag Root, Devil's Shoestring, Master of the Woods, Red Cayenne pepper and Black Pepper Powders. Used to confuse and destroy an enemy. **The Spell:** Into Hel's arms, I send you this night; confused you will be, at your unending plight! Destruction assured in each section of your life, let the cuts now run deep with my spellbinding knife!

Dipteryx Ordorata (Love Wishing Dreams): Tonka Beans, Apricot, Catnip, Elecampane, Orris root, Angelica, Honeysuckle, Jasmine and Saffron. Kept in a mojo around you, blown to the four directions, hung in a mojo on your bed or placed under your pillow is said to make your romantic dreams come true. **The Spell:** Love's Wishing Dreams, spun on a web, blown to the directions and hung on my bed; bring now the visions of love coming to me, plant in my mind the face I will see, draw them out at the same time you draw me, so our meeting by chance is met perfectly!

Kali's Destruction: Devil's Shoestring Root, Alum, Quassia Root, Couch Grass and Mullein powders. Used to stick and destroy an enemy. **The Spell Song:** My grandma and your grandma were sittin' by the fire; my grandma told your grandma, that man is such a liar! Your grandma told my grandma, we'll boogity him today, save your lovely daughter and, send him far away! Talkin' 'bout Hey now, hey now now, Kali's on her way, gonna come and strike that man right down, and make that sucker pay! Yeah, Hey Now, hey now now, Kali's on the way, gonna come and strike that man right down, and make that sucker pay!
Your grandma and my grandma were sittin by the fire, Your grandma told my grandma, that bitch is such a liar! My grandma told your grandma, we'll boogity her today, Save your grandson from her clutch, and send her far away! Talkin' 'bout, hey now, hey now now, Kali's on her way, gonna strike that 'ol bitch right down, and make that jezebel pay! Yeah, hey now, hey now now, Kali's on the way, gonna strike that ol' bitch right down and make that jezebel pay!

Einen Dieb Fangen (To Catch a Thief): Galangal, Hydrangea, Poke Root, Vetiver. Sprinkle around the scene of a crime to discover the thief. Then use a combination of mint, nutmeg and rose powders, and rub on your hands, shake hands with them and they have to tell you the truth! **The Spell:** Visions in my head may I see, the treacherous thief who did this deed! Open my senses so they may be found, a tracking spell, I lay on this ground! So whenever their face I now see, They must come and confess to me!

Luck of the Irish (Fast Luck): Cinnamon, Wintergreen, Ground Pyrite, and Vanilla Bean. Used to bring fast luck to any situation when needed. **The Spell:** Jack O the Green, Herne and Puck; send into my hands your endless luck! Bring it fast and make it strong, so it lasts all week long! 13X

Ghost be Gone: Basil, Rue, Purslane, Wild horseradish or Mustard seed, Rosemary, Woodruff and Broom. Used to get rid of entities. Can be put inside a pillow to prevent nightmares or used in a spray bottle for closets and under beds by children who suffer night terrors. **The Spell:** Ghost be gone, from this place, peace and safety I replace, take now your leave far from here, as I keep my Goddess near!

Goofer Dust: can be made from minerals, herbs, powdered roots, graveyard dirt, spider webs and their remains, dead flies or other bug corpses, harmful spices or poisons. The use of goofer dust is intended to harm, confuse, cross and sometimes kill a victim. Each recipe is and should be particular to the Witch, and circumstance for which it is used. Always be sure to feed your graveyard dust when adding it to any mixture. Typical ingredients may include sulfur, snake skin or heads, red pepper and/or black pepper, powdered bones, crushed insects and plant poisons. **The Song Spell:** Sitting by the crossroads, on a summers day, talking with my granny, passin' the time away; when a horseman passes, and to him I say, Goofer, goofer goofer, goober goober dee, take (name's) corpse with you, there hanging on the tree; I done drove him crazy, I done drove him mad, now down down into the grave, take this nasty lad!

Graveyard Dirt: Yes from an actual graveyard, not some plant. There is much to be considered here, as in, one must approach the graveyard with great respect and never disrespect the people there. Never walk on their gravesites, never sit upon their gravestones and never take without asking an leaving an offering. Many knock when entering a graveyard, whether on the gate or the ground, and if an ill feeling of foreboding comes over you, then don't enter. If you are given your pass then be prepared to greet the guests and give offerings. There are many graveyard mixtures to consider depending on your need. Nine soldiers is considered protective, as are Ancestors. Nine criminals are best considered for left hand work. Children are considered pure and helpful but one must consider how they died, as a murdered child can make a spiteful horrifying spirit. Always feed your graveyard dirt according to the moon cycles. Typical offerings range from 3 pennies or 9 dimes, to liquor, and tobacco for soldiers, honey and cakes or tea for women, to toys and sweets for children. Typical feed may be Powdered Sugar, Sulfur, Saltpeter or Salt. **The Song Spell:** In the graveyard, in the graveyard, when the moon begins to shine; Walking around, walking around, looking for a sign. Who here, who here, desires a bit of wine? To help me, to help me, a soul to spell and bind? What about, what about, these here silvers nine? To help me, to help me, a soul to spell and bind! (repeat until you find yourself the perfect partner).

Hot Foot Powder: Cayenne and Ground Black Pepper, with Iron Sulfate to stick it to them. You may also include goofer dust, sulfur, dirt dauber's nests (mud wasp) or graveyard dirt if you choose. Typically you would put it upon a path that they are sure to walk on, however these days, it works just as well on a vehicle door handle, by their steps, under their bed or mixed in a conjure ball and thrown on their roof or stuck in their bumper. **The Song Spell:** The wind is risin', the wind is risin', the leaves are trembling on the tree; I'm a sendin' a hell hound now, to come on after thee! The storms a risin', the storms a risin, it's fallin' down like hail, hellhound has your scent now, and he's fast upon your trail!

Lodestone Powder: Contains finely shaved and powdered Magnetic Iron Ore. Iron being a key element in protection from any spirit or evil intent. Used to draw Love, Luck, Money or Success to you. The Iron ore helps protect the spell form jealous eyes or disparaging spirits. If added to oil for a moon, then the oil can be used to dress candles. For mojo's place in a red flannel bag with your other ingredients. Lode stones themselves are typically fed with magnetic sand. **The Song Spell:** Draw, draw, draw, draw good love unto me; draw, draw, draw, a luck as fast as can be; draw, draw, draw, wealth and monies times three, draw, draw, draw, success in all I need!

Lucifer's/Enki's Seal: Lucifer the Morning/Evening Star of Light and Knowledge, Originally of the Ugaritic-Canaanites. Also known as the Trickster and of taking responsibility for your Magickal actions (as in if you choose to do selfish magick - and we all do – then do as you will as long as you don't impact another negatively without just cause). This should contain Solomon's Root, Lucky Hand Root, St. John's Wort, Star Anise, Galbanum and ground Crocosmia bulbs. Can be used in any situation to bring power and might to a spell, mojo, or a working. Especially good as a ritual powder. PS. Being cut off in traffic or having someone steal your parking space isn't just case, however, being bullied most certainly would be. **The Song Spell:** Luci-fer, Luci-fer, Enki, Enki, Enki; power and might, power and might, bring to me the key, Luci-fer, Luci-fer, Enki, Enki, Enki; untold success, untold success, in all I do and be!

Lucky 13 Lotto Powder: As its name suggests there are 13 ingredients for Luck, Money and Success: Lucky Hand, Dandelion, Dill, Hollyhock, Poppy, Rose, Star Anise, Honeysuckle, Cinnamon, Ginger, Linden Flower, with Bergamot and Nutmeg. Used as a wash on your hands or as a powder in your pocket, wallet or other place you would put a ticket. **The Spell:** 13 things to you I bring, to win the lottery; 13 things to ward success, and dispel all poverty! 13 things, I will share, when I win its true; 13 things is all I need for my life anew!

Lucky Hand Powder: Contains Salep which is a flour made from the tubers of the Orchid genus Orchis mascula or Orchis militaras, which is often contained in beverages or desserts in what was formerly the Ottoman Empire and spread to England and Germany. Often sweetened with Orange flowers or Rose water. Used for Luck in Gambling and to restore vigor to the Male sexual parts. If not using as a drink, you may desire to add some Magnetic Sand to it to attract Good Luck to it. **The Spell:** Lucky hand, lucky hand, of the glory be; lucky hand, lucky hand, bind good luck to me! Lucky hand, lucky hand, every opportunity, Lucky hand, lucky hand, open up for me! Lucky hand, lucky hand, I now hold the key, Lucky hand, lucky hand, of all that I can be!

Magnetic Sand: Magnetite or Iron Oxide shavings which are used to feed lodestones for the purpose of attracting Love, Luck, Money or Success. **The Spell:** Attraction sand, attraction sand, of good luck and power, bring all unto my open hands, all that I desire! Attraction sand, attraction sand, all good things that shall be, bring now unto my hands, and bind success to me!

Green Man of the Woods Powder: Master of the Woods Root, Galangal, Patchouli, Frankincense, Jasmine, Myrrh, Cinnamon, Mimosa and Sweet Almond Oil. Used to Master any Craft or Situation where you may need an upper hand. Great for Salesman, Tradesmen, Contracts etc. **The Spell:** Green man of the woods, Master of every fate; give to me the upper hand, and success create! Master of the woods, Known as the Greenman, in all contracts and agreements, grant me the upper hand!

Money Drawing: Allspice, Basil, Mint, Comfrey and Sweet Woodruff with Loadstone powder, and Magnetic Sand. Used to draw money to you. Put on top of unpaid bills, your check book or pay check stubs. Carry with you when asking for a raise, selling things, or keep in your desk at work. **The Spell:** Money draw, money draw, money come to me; money draw, money draw, wealth a plenty; money draw, money draw, untold success; money draw, money draw, that withstands every test!

Mutterseelenallcin (Forever Alone or Separation): Black pepper, Chili Powder, Cinnamon, Galangal, Iron Filings, and Vetiver with Hemlock oil. Used in the case of Divorce, Break ups (Personal or Business), or Contracts. Can be used on an Ex that won't leave you alone. **The Spell:** Mutter-seele-nall-cin, oh where do I begin? Separate and break, all contracts that were made; whether spoken or written laid, crush them and make them fade, upbraid and degrade, into decay so (name) has no reason to stay!

Salt: Used for protection and is a main ingredient in many washes and powders calling for protection against all manner of entities. Can also be used like Cascarilla powder to make circles or sigils on the ground while doing magickal rituals. **The Spell:** Protection and purity, this dear salt, grant unto me; keep me safe and protect me well, in every spell and ritual!

Sulfur: is a component of many minerals including iron pyrite, gypsum and galena. It can also be found as a byproduct of the petroleum industry. Care should be taken to wear gloves and a mask before collecting. It is yellow in color and often used for cursing, the feeding of graveyard dirt and for left hand work. Same as Brimstone. **The Spell:** Sulfur and brimstone, I bid you well, do your work, with my spell, whether a grave you feed, or summon a spirit for my need; I this moment empower thee, to do the deed, do the deed!

Sugar: Often called drawing powder (as it draws things to it, ants mostly, but if you put it on funnel cake it draws everyone!), Powdered or Confectioners' Sugar is always used to Sweeten peoples dispositions towards you or the situation at hand. Also generally used to clear the way for you in any situation as it makes you appear more likeable and agreeable to those meeting you. **The Spell:** Drawing Powder do so lead, all friend and foe to love me. Sweeten their dispositions so they will be, approving of my ideas and my deeds!

Sweet Magdalene or Stay With Me: Ground Rosemary, Bergamot, Spikenard, Myrrh and Patchouli. Used to keep a partner interested and to keep them from straying away from the relationship in any way. **The Spell:**

Sweet Magdalene, fidelity; is made of faith and chemistry; grant now these two things to me, so our love fills all our needs! Sweet Magdalene, bring to me, loyalty without jealousy, friendship always between he/she and me; grant this now, Mote it be!

Thor's Hammer Powder: A piece of a tree struck by lightning, bit of granite, a broken knife tip, swallow feathers, geraniums, and mistletoe. Bury in the southwest corner of your property or hang in a southwest window. **The Spell:** Thor, hammer of the Gods, protect my home and protect the sod; keep us safe from all lightning and storm, and each new morning let us be reborn!

Toten Ermorden Umbringen (Killing Powder): Graveyard dirt from an evil or murderous person, Asatifeda, Black Mustard Seeds, With either Salt and Snails powdered or Powdered Red Ants, Anvil Dust or Salt Peter, Sulfur or Gun powder, and the Black spores of a matured puff ball mushroom (commonly called devils snuff) with either mullein and valerian (Vandal Root) or the Seed pods of a Jimson Weed (commonly called a Devil's Apple)and powdered Dirt Dauber's Nest. Use the snails if you want the person to waste away and the salt peter or gun powder if you want to quicken the process or add strife. The asatifeda is used for potency. Vandal's root adds misfortune and an element of control. Anvil dust is so everyone will see the real ugliness or weakness of the person inside. Red ants, snake skin or blood brings poison into play. Ground owl bones will bring haunted dreams, while ground rat bones will bring a loss through theft, being ratted out or on, as well as fear and nightmares. Make on the New Moon and put in their foot prints on their door steps. Then blow into the four directions or for added intensity, place at every cross roads between them and the graveyard you desire to lay them in (as well as putting some in the graveyard as well). **The Song Spell:** 5, 4, 3, 2, 1; now let the awful deed be done; bloody murder in the night, the crows will sing of your plight, cawing from your outside stair, setting your name upon the air; from your bed to the graveyard be, (name, middle name) 1, 2, 3! (repeat)

UnWorting Powder (UnCrossing): Chili Powder, Galangal, Coconut, Lemon Grass, Hyssop, Rue, and Sage. Burn and pass yourself or the item through the smoke several times. Use after visiting a Graveyard or crossroads. May also be added or used as a mojo, bath or wash. **The Chant Spell:** Queen Boudicca, scream your battle cry, so all evil present will run and hide; Queen Boudicca, your warrior chant yell, send all curses against me to hell; Queen Boudicca, your army invade, unwort me from the curses that have been laid! (repeat)

Warding Powder: Brick Dust, Cast Iron Skillet Scrapings, Salt. For use with Bind Runes and Warding Spells. Also useful as a Ritual Powder or as a Floor Sweep or Wash, particularly in a Witchery or other Spiritual Center. **The Spell:** I raise up the Wards of power, getting stronger every hour; I raise them up in the North, a strong and impenetrable force! I raise them up in the East, to keep out every spirit and beast! I raise them up in the South, to shut down every gossiping mouth! I raise them up in the West, strong and fierce against every test! I raise them above, I raise them below, Keeping out ills words of friend and foe, and now I raise them from within, because sometimes I am my own worst friend! A Circle of Gold I spin around, keeping me safe upon the ground! A circle of silver I spin up high, keeping me safe when I fly! A circle of light I spin around me, keeping me safe wheresoever I be!

Witch's Domination Powder (Controlling): Calamus Root, Licorice Root, Honeysuckle vine, Couch Grass, Ginseng Root, Knot weed and Master of the Woods. Used to elicit necessary absolute control of a situation like over an abusive spouse or if one's life may be in danger. **The Spell:** Thence came the maidens, mighty in wisdom from down beneath the Yggdrasil tree; Mightily they wove the web of fate, while Bralund's town all trembling be! There the golden threads they wove, fast made in the Moon's hall, visions of terror and poison blades, none could escape, no none at all! On crystal and gold and goodly charms, on the nails of Norn's and the night owl's beak, I come upon the mists of time, for thy domination I now seek! Cursed you are and cursed you'll be, for now I call on the Valkyrie! For the Norns blessing or for the Norn's wrath, none can break free, of their woven path! As they send their ghastly hounds, you will hear them hunt you down! Upon the threads this spell dictates, the Three Norns have now sealed your fate!

How to Use a Powder: Sprinkle by stepping backwards (an odd number of steps or 7x7) to poison the feet of the intended victim, blowing into the four directions, or the four corners, or towards the person it is intended for; to double dress a candle (first with oil then with powder), Dusting or Dressing is done by putting your fingers in the powder and then making wavy lines upon something like a legal document or love letter; worn around the neck, in the pocket or in the bra next to the bosom; give as a gift to someone. Be careful if mailing because it could be thought to be hazardous and they could have the local Hazmat team out! So if you are going to mail, add to glitter of the same general color!

Different Dirt's used in Hoodoo: Please Note the Number 4 is used to correspond with the 4 Fold Goddess: Dirt From the 4 Corners is used to open up the roads of Success. Dirt from the Mountains is used in cleansing spells and Fairy Magick. Dirt from 4 Jails is used to either keep a person in jail or to release them. Dirt from 4 Police Stations is to either protect you from the law or to make the law aware of any criminal activity. Dirt from a Forest is used as a Ward in Protection spells. Dirt from 4 Banks is used for Prosperity Spells. Dirt from a Native American Cemetery has been used to help you find your Spirit Guide, Your Animal Guide, or as Protection if you are yourself Indigenous. Dirt from 4 Churches is said to be helpful in cleansing spells, but it depends on the Gods you hail. Dirt from the Motherlands is protective and a ward against invasion. Dirt from a Hospital or Doctors office can both be used to expel sickness or to bring it. Dirt from the Home of a Witch is often used in spells of requiring Domination. (Stop by for a Cup of Dirt and sit for a Spell anytime!). Dirt from a Mental Hospital is said to cause confusion and mental terror. Dirt from the home of a Priest of Santeria can be used in spells of protection. (but bring an offering to him). Dirt from a Courthouse or Law Library is said to win victory and favor in all Legal Matters and Court. Dirt collected at 12 noon and Midnight is said to be protective (I prefer 4am and 4pm). Dirt from a Seashore is used for Fertility and Cleansing Spells. Dirt from a Race Track or Casino is often used for Money and Gambling Spells. Dirt from a Rivers Edge is used for Love and Marriage. Dirt from the Bottom of your own shoes are good for spells of Domination and harm (Even better from the boots of a Witch!). Dirt from where two dogs have fought is good for spells of conflict. Dirt from a Soldiers grave is useful for spells of protection, domination and courage. Dirt from a Library is great for Knowledge and Wisdom spells, of course from the Library of Alexandria would indeed be phenomenal! (let me know if you get some!).

Reverse Curse Spell: You will need a candle that is red on one side and black on the other (light the black end). Dragons blood oil to dress the candle and Dragons blood incense to light. **The Spell:**

Red and Black send evil back, for it's been knocking at my door. Curse the one who so cursed me, to dwell in their wickedness as before! Let them see themselves clear as day, so they will mend their evil ways! Remove this curse when they are done, learning the lessons of compassion! This is my will for them to see, Lord and Lady, Now Mote it Be!

6 SWEEPS & WASHES

Sweeps are powder mixes used for sweeping evil away in the same means a Wash, washes it away when the powders are mixed with liquid. When using a broom, always sweep with an odd number to assure success. Some say 21 sweeps is best because it is 7 x 7 and 7 is supposed to be the number of the Spirit. I prefer 13 because it is the number of the Master. Scrubbing the front steps is often done to ward off evil, curses, and bad juju. Sweeps and Washes can also be used for bringing in good. Some of the mixtures provided would go well to set a moon, then remove the liquid to a spray bottle for use out of doors. Here are some great combinations:

Asgard's Blessing: German Chamomile, Heather, and Thyme; used while singing a prayer to dispel seasonal (or other) depression and bring peace as well as financial blessings to the household. **The Spell:** Gods of Asgard, Well of Urd, bind tight your blessings upon my word; as I sweep, so do you bless, my humble abode, my little nest; take away depression and fill it with peace; bring in wealth and make poverty decrease! Gods of Asgard, Well of Urd, Bind tight your blessings upon my word!

Alfheim, Svartalfheim and Nidavellir: Elder, Sweet Cicely and Fennel. Protective, used for discerning hope in hopeless situations, seeing the possibilities available amoungst the present limitations, understanding the hidden pain of a situation or finding a hidden disease or what is poisoning a person or situation. Also good for warding off fleas and ticks. **The Spell:** Open the windows, open the doors; give sight to my eyes to see to the core, reveal what is hidden with my spell, show me what others cannot tell!

Brighid's House Blessing: Mistletoe, Angelica, Ragwort, Fennel and Rue. Used to protect, bring fertility, heal, banish sickness and bring needed change to a household. Great when a new bride moves into first home. **The Spell:** May Brighid bless the house where we dwell, Every door, the land, the well; Bless each heart that resides within, Be they family or be they friend, Bless each girl, bless each boy, shower them with happiness and joy, bless each foot that passes through, May dear Brighid shelter them too!

Celt's Money Draw: Chamomile, Cedar, High John, Irish Moss and Buckeye. Wash your steps inwards for a continuous cash flow. **The Spell:** (add a silver coin or gold ring to the wash) Lovely Lady of the Moon, grant wealth to me very soon; fill my hands with silver and gold, all you give my stores can hold!

Cerridwen's Fiery Wall of Protection: Gunpowder, Brick dust, Broom and Cast Iron Scrapings. **The Spell:** The spell be cast in water and fire, a wall is buildt higher, higher; none shall pass this fiery wall, none shall pass except whom I call, let in only those who are willed by me, blind all others so my door, they cannot see!

Danu's Blessing: Lavender, Amber, Musk, Silver Magnetic powder with Ylang Ylang. Used to bless a home with good spirits, good luck, sweet dispositions and happiness. **The Spell:** A river is flowing, flowing, down to the sea; Mother of the Tuatha De Danann come bless me, a river is flowing, flowing, upon the earth; bring to me good spirits of luck and mirth; a river is flowing, flowing, from you to me, from all evil, set my house free!

Defender of Muspellheim: Stinging Nettle, Dragon's Blood and Cloves; used to protect and defend your household from unseen enemies of friends that would use you without mercy as it keeps away evil, averts danger, dispels ghosts and purifies the space. Drives away hostile forces, as it brings in prosperity and wealth to the household. **The Spell:** Stinging Nettle, Cloves and Dragon's Blood, drive away hostile forces in a flood; keep all who would harm at bay, sting their feet, burn their seat, and send them far away; avert all danger, dispel all ghosts, those who gossip, those who boast; from them all, purify this space, and bring to me wealth, in their place!

Dixie John (or Southern John): Trillium or Beth Root; keeps the home fires burning, bring in luck and money and keeps the family together. **The Spell:** Dixie John, Defender be, of this home and family, Bring in love, bring in luck, unstick us from the daily muck, keep each faithful in their turn, make the fiery passions burn!

Druid's Dryad: Vervain, Oak, Club Moss, and Mistletoe Powders. Used for Blessings and Border Protection inside and out. **The Spell:** Keepers of the wildlands, across the great deep sea, from the mists of Avalon, come now unto me! From the north, south, east and west; build my borders to stand each test, build them strong, build them tall. Make them stand against any thrall, from every direction that I see, then bring in blessings unto me!

Four Thieves: Rosemary, Sage, Lavender and Thyme (sometimes made with mint, clove, cinnamon, lemon or eucalyptus as well.) set in a Vinegar wash and used to cleanse a place and all furnishings of any sickness, disease or evil presence. Great when buying antiques or online. Completely edible for killing disease within. Especially good when boiling on the stove to kill any airborne disease so it doesn't spread. Great as a wash on any cuts after garden work. **The Spell:** Harken 4 thieves of Marseilles (Mar See); legend claims you hold the key, to kill each and every disease, and make every evil from you flee! So I spread you all across my floors, over the windows and around the doors, so presence or disease can be no more, and riches replace all that was once poor!

Hela's Banishing: Elder or Sycamore, Wormwood, Belladonna, Bittersweet, and Helebore. Used to banish spirits and entities into the outer realms. Warning: Never use as a sweep or a wash if you have pets or little children crawling around or playing on the floor because it is poisonous. However washing someone's clothes you intend to hex or sprinkling a Boogity is perfectly fine (just wash your hands after using please!).**The Spell:** Into the land of Jormundgrund, Hela bids you now to come, A place for you she has made, an great orchard she has laid, into her garden you must now go, because dear Hela herself, bids you so!

Helheim's Invisibility: Plantain, Amaranth and Fern; used to make you or your dwelling temporarily invisible or easily forgettable so someone won't be able to easily find it. As well this mix is restorative and protective for your spirit during astral travel and will help your spirit find safe return and passage even in the worst of situations. Also brings Good Luck to the household. Great for outdoor rituals. **The Spell:** Inside and out, I bid you all about, your eyes blinded they be, so none can see me! (take great care about doing this spell too often, as vehicles will literally run into you!)

Jotunheim's Hunt and Destroy: Viper's Bugloss, Witch Hazel, and Yarrow; Used to Hunt down Disease and Destroy it or, against people who are snakes in the grass. **The Spell:** Angrbroda, great goddess you be, send your children to come help me! Send them to destroy this dread disease! Send them now and set me free!

Lyn y Fan Fach: Meadowsweet, Cloves and Vervain used as a wash after a Funeral or before a Wake as a final tribute to the Departed Soul. **The Spell:** Dearest Hela, great goddess of the dead, for whom prepares an orchard to keep them duly fed, prepare now a special place, for my loved one to rest their head! Put aside for them a place, at your table there, allow them the peace and rest that you alone have prepared. Thank you dearest Hela, for your sacrifice, that keeps all souls happy in the afterlife! **Viking Funeral Prayer:** Lo there, So I see my Father; Lo there, So I see my Mother, and my sister and my Brothers. Lo there, So I see the line of my Peoples back to the beginning. Lo, They do call unto me. They bid me to take my place among them. In the Hallowed Halls of Valhalla. Where the Brave shall Live Forever! Skul! **Celtic Funeral Prayer:** Long is the day, and long is the night, and long is the waiting for Arawan. For the horses of

Donn, with our names written on, come to gather us in to his house. The horses be red, our fate now be dead, but our spirits be always be roused!

Midgard's Sanctification Wash: Mug wort with Pine Needles and Agrimony. Used to create Sacred Space, drive away demons, wild beasts, poisons and strokes; protects against possession, cures madness, clears the mind, heightens the senses and aides astral projection. Great for sanctifying any ritual wear or tools. **The Spell:** I have spun the circle wide, peace now within must abide, golden sphere surround my hide, for upon this night I will ride! Upon the mists of space and time, I set my presence, I release my mind, into the universe I now go, watch over body, here below!

Niflheim's Shift: Watercress with Angelica and China Berry; used to bring slow malleable change to convert a ridged situation or person to a more bendable or accepting one. **The Spell:** From the Niflheim, the source from whence all rivers come, change this ridged situation, into a more malleable one! Work your waters, as upon a stone, carving new ideas from their very bone! Slowly make them change, although they won't know why, to see the other side of the coin, and give new things a try!

Odin's Little Red Man: A combination of Poison Oak, Poison Ivy, Sumac, Holly berries and Ivy berries, crushed into a sweep or a wash as a means of sending the little red man of destiny after the person. Toss the sweep or wash on their front door, bedroom window, desk or vehicle. **The Spell:** Little Red Man of Destiny, May Odin come and set you free, take your army of phantom men, and trample (name) again and again! Spare them not a single thing, let the bells toll, for the death you bring! In this bag I lay your fee, 30 pieces of silver to do the deed! Now dear Odinn, set him free!

Orange Water: Orange, Bergamot, Ambergris, Orris root and vetiver. **The Spell:** Orange water of fidelity, let there always and forever be, perfect love and harmony, betwixt my spouse and me! Each day may the loyalty grow, each day kindness we will show, and each night in each other's arms, keep us safe from every harm!

Peace Water: Arrowroot, bayberry, sassafras, vetiver, lemon, lilac and rose with almond oil. **The Spell:** In this place where conflict be, bring now peace and harmony; let each one now finally be, understood for the things they see! Let each mind now embrace, and put each in the other's place! Let heart's now open, begin to mend, and love each other once again!

Protection Wash: Made on Moondays, Wodensdays and Freyasdays: get up at 4 AM and keeping silent, write the name of the local law enforcement commander on a paper and burn, then add this to a wash with your urine, and essence of van van, holy water, spring water or salt water, and wash your front steps. When dry, then sprinkle brick dust upon your steps for protection. Red brick dust is often mixed with paint for a protective measure of your porch and steps as well. All entrances into your home must be considered, even windows. **The Spell:** Dearest Loki come right now, and divert all against me with your tricks somehow. I leave the what and how up to thee, for when it comes to tricks, Thou Art a Mighty King, my Dearest Loki!

Vanaheim's Fertility: A mixture of Crab Apple, Fir and Silver are used to heal and strengthen the body to bring fertility to a home, person, field or herd of animals. **The Spell:** Once upon a time I felt a child within me, at that time it chose to leave, tell the child I am ready now, for upon this wash I take my vow, to be the best parent I can be, if you chose to come back to me! **Alternate Spell:** Once upon a time I felt a child inside me, at that time it could not be, tell the child I am ready now, for upon this wash I take my vow, to be the best parent I can be, if you chose to return to me!

War Water: Water from a Thunder storm or polluted source, set with 9 iron nails or coffin nails from moon to moon. Additions may include thorns of roses or honey locusts. Blood, Goofer dust, Urine, Red pepper or Gun Powder. Used for Protection, Battling Magick or Defense. **The Spell:** Morrigan, Morrigan, Great Washers at the Ford; upon this broom I place my oath, and thereby do I declare war! Be my battle maidens, Stand ye at my sides, Haunt their every dream, to my will abide! Ride forth in great terror, be ye not ignored, destroy them so completely, Great Washers at the Ford!

For Nettle Beer: (Why? Why not! Nettle beer has long been used as a health tonic especially when bridging the Croning stage of life!) In a large pot combine 2 gallons of cold water, 5 cups of washed, young Nettle leaves, 2 cups each of Dandelion leaves and Horehound or Meadowsweet flowers, 3-5 rhubarb stalks chopped, and 2 ounces of bruised Ginger root. Boil gently for 40 minutes, then strain and stir in 1 ½ cups of brown sugar. When cooled to lukewarm temperature, toast a slice of bread and spread with one cube of fresh yeast. Float the bread yeast side up on the top of the mixture, cover and allow to ferment for 24 hours. At the end of this time, open and remove the residue from the top of the beer. Add 1 tablespoon of cream of tartar and bottle as you would an ale.

7 CURIOS, OMENS AND CHARMS

Animals: animals, their fur, feathers, bones or skins can be used to bring luck, take it away, as a means of divination or even to acquire the abilities thereof, or shapeshift into the animal, providing you have a means of spirit communication with it. Many spells may require black cat or dog fur which is easily obtained by petting.

Avoiding Possession: to avoid possession one must wear black, haint blue or clothing with 7 colors stitched into it. You could also have mirrors sewn into your clothing or dust your body with cascarilla powder. Carrying Iron or a rowan cross made out of sticks and strings works well. As does wearing rose or lavender water. Throwing salt, seeds, or grains for the elves, demons or entities to count are a known deterrent as well.

Barn Quilts and Quilt Trails: For the Germans and the Norse, the first wand was the Distaff. Woman were honored for the magick they weaved into every stitch. They could weave in protection and blessings, or they could weave in a curse to have the first arrow strike you in battle. While there are many Battle Maidens and War Witches that joined the men on the field, there were also those at home left to care for the children, herds and land. They however were not so much left behind, as they were conjoined with their kinsman by weaving prayers into every stitch they sewed. Grown out of the Pennsylvania Dutch Hex signs, Quilt Trails were first started in Ohio to Honor a lost mother and the love she weaved into her quilt making for every member of her family, in her every stitch. Barn Quilts are a way of commemorating the Pioneer Woman by honoring their Ancestral Quilt Square. Many families have a particular quilt square that represents their heritage in their own set of colors. Others have been brought into being to represent a business or school that weaves in their skill or pride. Thus when you see an Appalachian Quilt Trail, think of all the prayers of protection that for thousands of years, were woven by each and every one.

Barn Signs or Hex Signs: (Hexafoo or Witches Foot) Are talismans or prayers made by the Pennsylvania Dutch as a form of Folk Magick that are related to images found in German Charm Books. All are a form of sympathetic magick or hoodoo and all the elements have meaning: For instance 4 pointed stars bring a bright day and 5 pointed stars conjure good luck. While the 8 pointed star conjures fertility and abundance. The Triple Star represent Success, Wealth and Happiness. A 16 pointed star brings prosperity (or double abundance), while a Maple leaf stands for Contentment. The Circle is for Eternity, Infinity and Protection. Two Distlefinks conjure Love, Happiness in marriage, where one is for Good

Luck and Love. The Dove represents Peace and Contentment while the Horse Head Protects animals from disease and the barn from lightning. The Eagle stands for Good Health, Strength and Courage while the three Tulips represent Faith, Hope and Charity. A Bird of Paradise is Welcome and Hospitality. Rain Drops bring Abundance, Fertility and Rain which produces good crops while the 4 quarter moons represent the four major seasons of the year. The 12 pointed Rosette and stars of a Daddy Hex ward off famine and bring good luck and joy all year round. Oaks and Acorns bring strength; wards off sickness and disease, as well as bestowing, longevity. Rosettes conjure Good Luck, Keep bad luck and evil at bay. Hearts of course for Love and Kindness (for without kindness there is no love). The Crowing Cock wards off evil. The Heifer brings fertility for the herd. The White Unicorn stands for Virtue, Piety and belief in God, but if they are black they will bring ruin to the household. The Waves outside of an image represent smooth sailing in life.

Barn Stars: Like barn signs, barn stars came over with the Pennsylvania Dutch and originally had six points (Sechs became Hex) They are to bring a family or herd protection and Luck. Originally made of wood, they are now made of metal and you can get them almost anywhere. All colors have meaning. Black means protection, and is used to bind the elements together. Brown represents the Mother Earth, but can also mean friendship and strength. Blue represents protection, peace, tranquility and the spirit. Green represents growth, fertility, success and is used for all things you desire to grow. Yellow represents Father Sun, Health of Body and Mind and Charity. Orange stands for Abundance, and the increase of a Career or the culmination of a Project. Red represents action, creativity, charisma, passion and intensity in emotion. Purple stands for all things Sacred. White represents the Moon, Purity, and unblocks the flow of energy.

Bannock Cake: for a maiden to see the face of the man she will marry, she must bake a bannock cake in the evening. Then in complete silence, wrap it in a cloth bearing her desire, walk it into her room, and place it under her pillow. She will then see his face in her dreams and if she looks carefully, other things that will represent a time line. In the morning she is to eat the bannock cake to secure the lines that will bring him to her.

Beans: St. Joseph Beans aka Wishing Beans. Tonka Beans aka Love Beans, You must make an odd number of Wishes (1, 3, 7) and for each wish put a bean in your pocket. Carry them for 7 days and then go to a river or running water and say: **The Spell:** To the River (Sea) I go and 3 times I knock, Once for Odin, Once for Thor and Once for Lok, Grant me the graces for whence I came, In the lovely Freya's Name! Note: Beans can also be used as a filler in a Boogity or to bring luck to a household.

Bells and Chimes: have from the beginning of time been used to deter ghosts and spirits away from a place or property. That is why they are rung before mass in temples and churches and prior to doing rituals and spells. Of course hanging windchimes makes sure to keep spirits at bay every time the wind blows!

Besom: Still in some parts of the Appalachia, you can find a corn broom with a woven top. This is always the broom used to dispel evil. Whether in your home or in your circle. Depending on where you came from, your standing in the coven or what's available, your besom can be made of many different things. In the Appalachia what stands out is that the top of our besoms are always woven, and sing song prayers are often included in their making.

Blackbirds, Crows and Ravens: Well prized as the messengers of the dead, as well as the messengers of Odin, Morrigan and Hekate. Always give them an offering if you can, when so ever they talk to you to thank them for their service. Even if your mind doesn't grasp the message, your spirit will. If however a blackbird comes and takes something from your porch or steps and then caws, it is said that a death will occur in the family. As well if it nests on your windowsill. The only way to stop it is to retrieve the item. If a Raven nests on your roof then death will occur in a fortnight, unless they are scared away while you are silent and still (consider sticks, stones, cats and even gun shots but never kill one). Crows warn of a blight on your land, misfortune or famine to come, so prepare by stocking up, buying seeds and making sure you have enough canning equipment.

Black Cat Bone: Now these can only ever be truly gotten through a cat who has lived a long happy life, otherwise they won't grant you the magick.. They are then buried and the bone removed in a years' time. One of the bones will have a bit of a knob, be bitter tasting and wont reflect in a mirror. This bone is said to grant invisibility, good luck, protection from malevolent magick, rebirth after death, and romantic success.

Blue Color (Haint Blue): Prized in all cultures, on all continents, and in all ages as being protective. Used in beads, around doors and window panes, on ceilings, in jewelry, clothing, religious wear, barn signs, etc. Now exactly what shade is haint blue? Well some will say turquoise, others will say lapis, however in truth it is the shade of blue that disappears in the dark. Yes there are a couple different shades of blue that are even harder to see than black is in the dark. These are Haint Blue. The idea being if we can't perceive them, then evil can't either. Therefore haint blue makes you or whatever you paint invisible to evil. Go ahead, do a few experiments on a new moon and see which is harder to see, it will indeed surprise you!

Blue Bottles: Prized throughout the Appalachia as being able to turn back a neighbors jealousy or the evil eye. Often found inverted (laying upside down) on bottle trees or hung in trees for this purpose. The idea is that they can capture the curse sent and destroy it with the rising sun. They are also kept in chimneys so it captures any evil that might that way come and send it back up with the smoke of a fire. Some are even put in closets or kitchen cupboards to capture any evil or curse sent. It is said they can get in, but can't get out. Sometimes you need to brown bag these ones and bury them or leave them in the sun for a few days.

Filled with spring water, blue bottles can be used to make Holy Moon Water, Altar Water and Healing Water. This works because water changes and attunes to different energies and vibrational frequencies, as does color. I personally keep a blue bottle filled with water by my bedside, near to the Himalayan salt lamp. The salt lamp sends out positive ions into the water that I then drink up every morning!

Blue Solar Water is very popular in Ho'o pono pono and used to heal deep emotional wounds and to free one's self from blocks and outdated programming. Just like Moon Water, fill the bottle with natural spring water, leave open and out in the Sun for at least an hour before consuming, better yet put out when you wake and claim before the sun goes down.

Most Witches Bottles are blue, but with your own tag locks so the evil sent to you gets trapped instead.

Bluing: There is two types of bluing: One for washing fabrics and One for cleaning guns and steel, both are considered protective and often hung behind doors, in chimneys, hidden in corners etc. to cleanse the area and protect the occupants. Same as with the aforementioned blue bottle only with a bit of liquid inside so they suffer.

Boogity: also referred to as a Doll Baby or a Poppet, can be made from anything including a corn husk, cloth, clay, leather, rope, feathers, roots, sticks, twine, wax or even metal. We have an entire book on this entitled the Art of the Boogity and so wont delve any father with it here.

Children: are protected by hanging a mojo containing yarrow and pixie lichen moss by their beds to keep curses and evil at bay. They can also be fed chamomile in their milk at night to calm them, protect them from evil and preserve their life. Prayers are often written and tucked into their pillow or mattress for protection as well. If you have a child with night terrors, it is because they can perceive what you can't. Dowse their room, move their bed accordingly and put down copper rods and mojos as needed.

Clay: is used in exorcism and dispersing spirits because it draws out poisons from the skin, like insect bites and poison ivy. However, it also cleanses from within. Bentonite Clay expels heavy metals and toxins from the body. In fact, all over the world (not just here in the Appalachia) people eat clay when they are sick and it does indeed work! In fact it cleanses the colon and liver, balances the bacteria in your intestinal tract, improves the assimilation of nutrients into the body and strengthens the immune system. It has been shown to eliminate food allergies, food poisons, burns, diaper rash, colitis, viral infections, parasites; treats arthritis, cataracts, diabetic neuropathy, pain, wound, diarrhea, stomach ulcers, bites, acne and alcoholism! Best part is it protects the body against radiation and should be used before and after any cancer treatments. Make sure you are going for the right kind of clay, but then stock up, because it's cheap and effective against everything!

Coins: Copper Coins can be used as "Coppers" for protection or Indian Head Pennies as Indian Scouts or Look outs and also used in Law Keep Away spells (must be a coin before 1982 to be copper). Silver Mercury Dimes to pay Helpful Spirits for their service (9 dimes is customary, 30 for a death) and for spells for business or commerce as well as being able to turn evil back to the sender (the dime will turn black if you have been cursed). 2 dollar bills or queer Money (Monopoly Money) is used for business spells and often shredded on mason jar and prosperity rice spells. Confederate Dollars or Silver Certificates can be used for destroying someone's business or for taking someone's money away. Now remember, never pick a coin that is face down, because it's bad luck, but put that face up penny in your pocket for a rainy day!

Containers: honey jars, amulet cases, picture frames, candle holders, boxes, jars, bottles, vials, coconuts, leather or cloth bags, clay pot and more can be used for various spells for innumerable purposes.

Crossroads: a crossroads is not where two roads cross (this is a common misconception), but where one road ends into another. Think the letter Y or the capital letter T. So technically, most driveways (since the invention of such) are crossroads. Something to consider when cursing someone. A good magick to consider for a crossroads is the making of a set of keys. Take two skeleton keys that resemble each other as much as possible, tie them together with a red string that measures from your heart to the wrist of your left hand (as this is most used for left path magick). Now tie them to your left wrist with the red string and keep them with you from new moon to new moon, making sure that they get as much of you on them as possible. At the end of the month, on the new moon, go to a crossroads, cut the string and use one key to dig a hole to bury the other. Sing **The Spell:** Hekate, Hekate, Crossroads Queen, grant me passage whenever I need! 13X (you may consider leaving an offering as well). You now have a key to the crossroads that can be used anytime!

Curse Bottle: red brick dust, 9 navy beans, 9 rusty nails, name paper of the intended victim, and moonshine: shake well and curse them to hell. Then throw into a sewer.

Cutting: Cutting a string of knots or the use of scissors or knife in a spell is a form of banishment. It can be used to sever a tie or bond between people or to cut away the pain or sickness from them. Take a length of red, black or silver cord and tie a knot at one end representing yourself. At the other end visualize a person who has been mean to, or a person that has attacked you in some way (or how a disease has torn at you). As you envision, tie a knot. Now keep the vison and tie 8 more knots (9 in total on the opposite end of your knot). Visualize all the wrong this person as done to you (or the disease has put you through) and **Speak:** Between you and me, this hex I break, for this hex never was right for you to make; now it's path I abruptly end, and back to you this hex I send! Now cut the cord between your knot and all the other knots and leave them at a crossroads without looking back by taking 9 steps backwards, throwing salt across your tracks so you can't be followed and singing nonsense songs, then take a salt bath after.

Dice: Can be read as a style of divination on its own called Cleromancy as discussed on page 7 in our book The Art of Divination, or as Numerology as discussed on Pages 149-159 of the same book.

Distaff: The original wand used by women to weave spells and prayers into everything they sewed. Think on it, if you put together every stitch in your house, and you wove your magick into every stitch, how very protected you would be from all manner of things. Perhaps all the disease today is not simply that many forget how to grow and preserve their own food, but that many forget how to preserve themselves by making a simple stitch.

Doors: A saucer placed above your door offers protection against thieves just like dried leather beans hung over a door bring in luck and prosperity. Iron over your door protects against fairies and spirits. Mistletoe offers the protection of the Druids and protects against sickness and disease. Onions hung at midnight on New year's eve bring prosperity and divert evil.

Eggs: Although we have an entire chapter dedicated to the egg, here we will note that it can be used to divine whether you will find love in the year to come or not. Simply hold an egg or rub it on your body asking for it to see for you, then separate it and drop the yolk into a glass of water. If it floats then love will come, if it sinks then friendships will hold you up until the fates are more giving.

Evil Eye: Known across all cultures as a blue bead or eye that can turn back evil. Also known is to give the evil eye is well an intense stare making a sign with your fingers as a horn or with your thumb set between your middle and ring fingers and thrust out. Once an Evil Eye is made or obtained prayers: **the Exorcism of the Eye:** (Carmina Gadelica, Sacred Texts) I trample upon the Eye, As tramples the duck upon the lake, as tramples the swan upon the water, as tramples the house upon the plain, as tramples the cow upon the pasture, as tramples the Host of the Elements, As tramples the Host of the Elements. Power of the Wind I have over it, Power of Wrath I have over it, Power of Fire I have over it, Power of Thunder I have over it, Power of Lightning I have over it, Power of Storms I have over it, Power of the Moon I have over it, Power of the Sun I have over it, Power of the Stars I have over it, Power of the Firmament I have over it, Power of the Heavens and of Worlds I have over it, Power of the Heavens and of Worlds I have over it. A portion of it upon the Grey Stones, a portion of it upon the Steep Hills, a portion of it upon the Fast Falls, a portion of it upon the Fair Meads, a portion of it upon the Great Salt Sea, for she herself is the best instrument to carry it, the Great Salt Sea, the best instrument to carry it! In the Name of the Three of Life, In the Name of the Sacred Three, In the Name of all the Secret Ones, and of the Powers Together! **Spell for Evil Eye:** The fair spell that lovely Mary sent, Over the stream, over sea, over land, against incantations, against withering glance. Against inimical power, against the teeth of wolf, against the testicles of wolf, against the three crooked cranes, against the three crooked bones, against the three crooked 'creothail, and against the lint 'leothair' of the ground. Whoso made to thee the eye, May it lie upon himself, may it lie upon his house, may it lie upon his flocks, may it lie upon his substance, may it lie upon his fatness, may it lie upon his means, may it lie upon his children, may it lie upon his wife, may it lie upon his descendants. I will subdue the eye, I will suppress the eye, and I will banish the eye. The three arteries inviting suffering, and the tongue of death completely. Three lovely little maidens, born the same night with Christ, is alive be these three tonight, life be a near thee, poor beast!

Feathers: Wing feathers can be used as Quill Pens with magickal Ink for writing spells. Black Feathers can be used for cursing by spelling the feather and placing it or by tying it to an old piece of clothing of the victims. Witches Ladders typically use found feathers for wishing spells and black feathers for protection.

Hag Stones: A Hag Stone is a stone with a hole in it, often found near a water source like a river, stream or the ocean. These can be carried for good luck, hung above a bed to prevent nightmares, suspended in a vehicle to prevent accidents or even attached to a backpack to prevent bullying.

Haint: A spook, ghost or wandering spirit who isn't happy. Typically found in haunted places, as they are attracted to abandoned buildings, in particular ones where people have suffered in, like jails and mental hospitals. Can also be found if a person was murdered, raped or abused in an area.

Hair: Hair must never be cut except on a New Moon or Growing Moon if it is to continue to grow. My daughter calls this the bane of Appalachia, as she is the only kid she knows that has to argue with her Mum as to what phase the moon is in before she is permitted to get it cut!

Hand of Glory: Is the dried and pickled left hand of a man that was hung for murder. It is cut from the criminal then pickled in salt and the urines of a man, woman, dog, horse and a mare. It is then smoked with herbs and hay for a month, hung on an oak tree for 3 nights (some say 9 like Odin) then laid upon a crossroads; hung on a church door overnight (while the maker keeps watch on the porch). If then, no fear has driven them away from the porch, then the hand is true and you have won it over. It is then used with a candle made from the fat of his corpse and invoked by saying "Now open lock, to the Dead man's knock! Fly, bolt, bar and band, Move according to the Dead Man's hand! All inside don't move or swerve, a single joint, muscle or nerve, all are at my command, within the spell of the

Dead Man's hand! Sleep all who sleep, wake all who wake, but be as the dead for the dead Man's sake! When invoked it is said to make everyone who sees it motionless and thereby powerless. Some say the best Hand of Glory is Mandrake Powder blown into the face of the person or persons you desire to control.

Honey Jar: of all the containers available, the best one is always a honey jar, although a molasses or syrup jar works in a pinch. Spells that need sweetened are placed inside, like a court mojo or name papers and baby dolls of people not getting along (small ones in big jars). Spells for employment, or for a work contract to sweeten the deal are also put inside. I keep a 5lb honey jar by my altar for all the spells I need sweetened!

Horse Shoes: Revered in many cultures as lucky and able to repel evil. It is said in some cultures it must be pointed up so the luck doesn't run out and to point down brings bad luck, however, In others it must be pointed down so the luck pours out upon you. The horse shoe must always be used and found to be considered lucky. Saint Dunstan, a blacksmith by trade is said to have been given the task of shoeing the devil's Steed and instead shoed the devil himself! This causing the devil much pain, he agreed to never enter a place where a horseshoe is hung over the door if St. Dunstan removed it from him, and thus why it is said to repel evil!

Inks: Named for the sympathetic magick the herbs used possess: Dragons Blood for Gambling, Money, Power, Contracts, Blessings and Protection. Dove's Blood is used for Love spells, Fidelity Spells, Romance, Passion and to Bring back a lost love. Bat's Blood is for use in Destruction Spells, Curses, Revenge and Dark Magick.

Iron: Considered able to keep away and destroy evil, repel or contain ghosts, fairies, or malevolent spirits. An iron horseshoe repels evil and brings luck. Burying an iron knife under the entrance of your home is said to keep evil and thieves out. Iron gates around cemeteries were thought to keep in the souls of the dead (in the case of vampires or the wandering spirits). Exorcism Knives throughout the centuries have been made with solid iron, often with a prayer, rune or sigil engraved upon them. So move over Silver, Iron has you beat hands down! From three rusty iron nails carried in a mojo or medicine bag to railroad spikes wrapped with copper wire and obsidian to keep away the Djinn, Iron in any manner and use has always been used as an instrument to keep evil at bay! Iron above your doors and fireplace keeps the fairies out, who incidentally tend to cause quite a bit of mischief otherwise and are known for stealing children and replacing them with a changeling.

Keys: Are used in bone divination sets and worn or carried in mojo bags to open up the doors of opportunity or to unlock bound or locked up situations . They can also be hung on Witches Ladders or Spirit Trees for the same reason.

Kitchens: The Kitchen is considered the Heart of the home and prior to having separate rooms for everything, the hearth/fireplace was located in the kitchen. So many hearth spells also work very well in a kitchen especially if your home doesn't contain a fireplace. Hanging a braid of garlic in your kitchen wards against illness while keeping a basil plant there brings prosperity.

Knocking: Knocking three times is said to avert ghosts and evil and protect the knocker. This comes from **the spell:** Three times on the door I knock, Once for Odin, Once for Thor and Once for Lok! This spell is also used when hanging horseshoes for luck and protection. Three knocks are be struck on the ground or gate of a cemetery before entering to ask the spirits permission to enter, on the door of a home before entering so no evil befalls you within, and on your bedpost before going to sleep so you are not plagued with nightmares or are not plagued with visits from inkkubus or sukkubus.

Knots: Tying a knot on the left side of a shirt or dress can tie up any evil sent against you. In fact knots are often used to curse or uncurse someone. In a string measured in your size, fold it 3 or 4 times, tie a knot at one end representing you and then tie nine knots at the other end representing anything that vexes you (disease, poverty, depression, etc.). Now cut the string between you and them and toss out at a crossroads.
Another good knot spell is to face and turn in each of the four directions 3x times and tie 4 knots saying **the spell:** I knot you knot, I bind you bound, All poverty sent here is thus turned around! All evil sent now sinks to the ground, and only Prosperity can now be found! Now go bury it where you wouldn't normally pass by, taking all precautions as you do.

Lucky Nuts: Many nuts are carried for Luck or Healing of Rheumatism or to Ward of the Chills. Some of these are Buckeye, Nutmeg, Brazil, Walnut, and Horse Chestnut.

Madstone: A common treatment for poisonous bites, and particularly rabies, was the use of the 'madstone.' A madstone is a small calcified, porous substance, usually oval-shaped, said to be found in the stomach of animals. Such a stone, taken from a white deer, was said to be of great value. Because of the porosity of the madstone, it readily absorbed liquid. It was first placed in a pan of warm water or milk, then applied to the affected part. If the stone stuck, the wound definitely held poison. The absorbed liquid often turned green, which indicated the poison was being drawn out. It was returned to the pan of warm liquid and applied to the wound again and again, until it no longer stuck to the wound. When this happened, all poison is said to be withdrawn.

Measuring: the use of measuring a person with a string is very useful in sympathetic magick when you are doing a spell for another as it can represent the person you are doing the magick for. The string can also be used to convey protection in your name, like a mother or grandmother may make weave a bracelet for a child with a measure string from each one to keep the child safe when coming and going from school.

Medicine Bags: Hung on the neck like a necklace and used as good medicine for protection of the Body, Mind and Spirit. Each is particular to the person and often contain healing herbs, crystals, a symbol of their Spirit Animal and things found in walkabouts. Therein is often also contained the Three Sisters (Corn Kernel, Bean, Squash Seed) and symbols of the four elements (shell for water, feather for air, flint for earth, opal for fire). Sage for the Sky God and Fir or Pine Needles for the Earth Mother.

Mirrors: (Unbroken) round convex mirrors are said to reflect back curses and jealousy sent to you. Put one that can be seen just left of the entrance to your home, office space or room. NOT directly as then Money in, Money out. (Broken) to avert the 7 years bad luck take the largest shard to the cemetery and touch it to the oldest headstone at midnight. Broken mirror pieces are often put in Witches Bottles to confuse spirits. As well when someone passes into the next realm, all the mirrors in the house must be covered for 4 days, so they can't linger, possess or haunt you!

Mojos: Spell pouches, many are Haint Blue or Red to avert the spirits from interfering with your spell. Others are colored according to the purpose.

Moss: Crush garlic and rub it on a strip of moss to cover and heal a wound up. Irish moss (not a real moss) is considered very lucky.

Name Papers: have a long tradition in all magick. Whether it be your own name to bring blessings upon, or the name of an enemy to bring curses upon, they are often very important for directing a spell. Name papers can also be petitions or spells that are attached to candles or put in a shoe (to ground the intention). They can be inserted into bottles, amulets and other containers to maintain a persistent influence on the situation.

Nine Irons Charm: carried by farmers and workmen for Luck, Protection, Healing, Curse breaking, and Keeping away Evil Spirits and Fairies. The Nine charms are made of iron by a blacksmith and are hung on the belt during the day and hung over the bed at night. The skillet was heated to red to ward off enemies, the saw and ax ward off evil spirits. The plow coulter and plow share are said to sooth children who have trouble sleeping (I can attest to this). The shovel and spade enable one to find stolen and lost property. The cross is used to bless holy water, and to protect from evil spirits. The horseshoe is for good luck and the anvil is for a good marriage as people were often married by the blacksmith over the anvil.

Passing: A means of a person passing through a threshold or back forth through people has well been used by all in sympathetic magick. For instance carrying a bride through the threshold of the door denotes fertility upon the couple. Passing through the spilt trunk of a lightning struck tree will cause all bad luck to be split from you. Passing a sick person back and forth between two strong healthy ones will throw the sickness off them and convey strength and good health to return.

Potatoes: Potatoes have been used for all types of magick. You can rub a wart with one on a full moon and bury it and the wart is said to fade away with the moon. You can write a wish on them and bury them,(on the new moon) then the wish will grow as the potato plant grows. If the plant doesn't grow then your wish hasn't been granted. You can present a plate of cooked potatoes to the spirits at night (announce they are for the spirits), then bury before the dawn and the spirits will be stuck to the potatoes and never bother you again. If you know the identity of the spirit then take a unwashed, unpeeled blue potato, slice it in half, carve out a small hole in each side being careful to leave thick solid walls, place a tiny object belonging to the spirit inside, seal it together with 2 long thin nails or pins and place it in the graveyard. The spirit will then be bound to the cemetery. A slice of raw potato will also take the pain and redness out of a burn.

Porches: Can be painted haint blue or with red brick dust added to the paint in order to avert evil As well you can plant fern, ivy and dill to protect against animals and curses. If however the plants do get eaten, it's a sign that a curse has already been placed and further measures must then be taken.

Rabbit: A rabbits left hind foot is lucky, as long as it is captured in a graveyard at midnight by a man with black hair (supposedly the grave keeper or a thief depending on the kind of luck you desire)

Red Color (Venetian): A type of barn red that is made of an iron oxide pigment called Venetian Red. It is important to note that the color Red is associated with Blood and Sacrifice, it is the Iron Oxide in it that says that Never may you take blood and sacrifice from my door. IF HOWEVER, you are just painting your door any old red, without the iron oxide, then you are INVITING EVIL TO USE YOU AS A BLOOD SACRIFICE!

The Red Corn Stalk: Pluck will I the little red stalk of surety, the lint the lovely Bride drew through her palm, For success of health, for success of friendship, for success of joyousness; For overcoming of evil mind, for overcoming of evil eye, for overcoming of bewitchment, for overcoming of evil deed, for overcoming of evil conduct, for overcoming of malediction, for overcoming of evil news, for overcoming of evil words, For success of blissfulness, for success of blissfulness! Then hang the red corn stalks in the kitchen.

Rhymes: are said to possess great power as they are meant to confuse the spirits and get them lost in the sing song of the words. Many spells therefore have their power increased by the rhyming of words.

Salt: When salt is spilled it must be quickly tossed over the left shoulder and thrown into the eye of the devil to be rid of him.

Shells: The Gold Ring Cowrie is often used in divination, to represent the Goddess, or Worn as a amulet. They are used in spells for prosperity, or used as a means of divination. In the bone set it can represent the Female. Bee Shells are said to manifest wishes. Cat's Eye Shells to ward off evil and for hex protection. Razor Shells can be used to help a Medicine Woman gather a lost piece of a person's spirit in the netherworld and blow it back into them in this world in order to heal them.

Shoes and Curse Deterrents: It is common to place an old shoe of every member of the household under the front steps, or buried by them to deter curses who have been sent against you. The curse will find the shoe and stick to it instead. Witch's Bottles work the same way. As does carrying a lock of your hair, a stick from your yard and a nail clipping wrapped in red string. It is also well to point the toe of the shoe in towards the house so they are coming home, not leaving. So that even when they are older they will always visit and remained tied to the family.

Singing: The Northern Gods and Goddesses were always sung to as a means of honor and benediction. The level of ability your voice is capable of, is of no matter whatsoever. It is only the intent and power for which the song comes from that counts, as in that which lies deep within your heart.

Smudging: While the use of sage is very prominent for smudging, you may consider the old Appalachian way of using valerian root, basil and rue to purge any and all evil from the premises. Traditionally the eldest child or child with the darkest hair does the smudging while the youngest walks behind with a candle to represent the Goddess Brigid.

Snakes: It is said the St. Patrick drove the snakes from Ireland. It is meant that he drove out the Pagans by conversion or death. Snakes are associated with Eternal Knowledge and the rising of the Kundalini. The Druids were considered knowledgeable on all matters, especially healing. The Christian Church made money off of spiritual healing. They even went so far as to sell chicken bones as Saint relics (thus why it is heretic for an Appalachian American to use chicken bones in divination). Even in their bible, it is the Snake (aka Bard) who tempts Eve into eating the apple (aka having Sex, thus acquiring Carnal Knowledge). It is then Adam who sees and desires the apple (aka Sex) from Eve. Thus why the Sons of Abraham say they are tainted and incapable of controlling their own body and minds around a woman. Druids however, lived by a code of ethics, that called for a person to be in control of their actions and to answer for them. Thus the Fallen Angels are the Old Gods who taught mankind the Divinations and workings of Nature and so the Church of Greed and Lies called them evil and sought to destroy them and all they stood for. Even if it meant killing every Wise Woman (Inquisitions) and destroying your memory of the Warrior Goddesses so you wouldn't rise up against them. Sheep are so much easier to control. Thus why Psalm 23 is really about the Wise Shephard that brings back a destroyed penitent sheep who acquired knowledge back into the fold as an example. In fact all the psalms are about being a good slave, in penitent petition to your master. So are you a slave or are you the snake people, who crossed an ocean and hid your knowledge of the workings of the vibrations of the earth and all its creatures, by talking to snakes in church? Because you see, snakes don't bite snakes, however, they will seek and attack a false person! Therefore be True of Heart; let the Kundalini within you Awaken and Rise up like the True Warriors you are!

Spirit or Bottle Tree: Used all over the Appalachia to capture or divert spirits of all kinds (depending on the bottle color). The most usual color is blue to avert the evil eye. The entire spell is in our book The Art of the Boogity on page 17. The most important thing to remember is that the bottle must be inverted (upside down) with the insides unwashed so it still contains an essence of the liquor to entice the spirits to be trapped within.

Spit: I don't know about you but in my day spit cured everything. The thing was the spit had to be from a woman who bore three healthy children. I read a science paper on blood once and contacted the guy who wrote it telling him that spit from a woman who born three healthy children was a cure for wounds. He probably laughed but he looked into it, and sure enough a woman who bears three healthy children, retains the extra antibodies in her blood and her spit. Now guess what! Women who have borne three healthy children, are especially prized for giving blood for transplant patients! Yep, they did an extra study after the spit one and now it's a question they ask on the form you fill out before you give blood! Thanks to my Granny, and all the Appalachian folk like her, now less people will reject their transplants! Ah now get on up, let me put some spit on that for yah!

Tag Locks: can be nail parings, hair, menstrual blood, semen, sputum, perspiration, tears, urine, feces, salvia (cigarette butts), dust from a foot print, handwriting on a piece of paper, or clothing once worn, and are used to target a spell.

Three for Bane: (the Cursed Number) It is often said that all bad things including deaths or accidents come in threes. So whenever something is failed twice, it is most unlucky to try again. Therefore another method or route must be taken or it must be left undone.

Troll Cross: actually considered a new addition to Appalachian Hoodoo, its idea was indeed born of the Old Ones blood. A troll cross is typically made of iron to repel all evil and made to resemble the rune Othala to protect you, your linage, your home, your property and your monies as well. A friend of mine, Marvin Lee Billings, lives in Tennessee and is a great and powerful artisan. When his home burnt down, the first item that came out of his new shop was a Troll Cross that still sits upon his neck to this day. So when my home got lost in a forest fire, my first thought was to have him make Troll crosses for my daughter and I. Ours are a little more fancy, bathed in silver and with mother-daughter stones, but they never leave our necks! You can find his magickal wares under Spice Dragon on Etsy.

Wadjet/Eye of Ra/Eye of Horus: Used a symbol of protection, wisdom and revelation. Reversed it is seen as subjugation, control of knowledge, illusion, and the manipulation of power.

Witch Balls: much like bottle trees and spirit trees, witch balls entice the wandering spirit to come in by their bright colors, thus capturing and giving it safe haven (like a skull on your altar gives safe haven to a spirit). Some say that once the sunlight dawns and hits the ball or bottle that the wandering spirit is then destroyed.

Wood: Acorns protect against hail, while Oak strengthens the home against natural disasters. Pine and Cedar bring prosperity. Birch brings happiness and elm protects against curses. Rowan commands spirits back to their place and makes a good border in the four corners of your property.

Writs for Rats: The caretaker of the house must first write a letter to the vermin who have chosen to infest your home. Ask politely for them to depart and to make their home elsewhere. The writ must recommend where elsewhere is, exactly how to get there (if they need to cross a river then a log must be provided), and why going to this other location is advantageous (like an unlimited food source). Put as many rhymes in it as you can. The Master of the house must then read the letter out loud to the rats. It is then greased in lard or butter (a few plant powders may be added mixed with sugar). Then rolled into a ball and put it down the rat hole. Some Rats will leave quickly, others may need more convincing.

The Teapot Song: Thou art the Vessel, I am the Fire; overflow my cup with all I desire! Thou art the Vessel, I am the Earth, overflow my cup with Merriment and Mirth! Thou art the Vessel, I am the Sea, overflow my cup and, make me all I can be! Thou art the Vessel, I am the Sky, overflow my cup and make my Spirit fly! Thou art the Vessel, I am the Air, overflow my cup with, Treasures rare! Thou art the Vessel, I am the Tree, find me the perfect one to Love and Care for me!

8 BIND RUNES & TAROT SPELLS

Bind Runes: A Bind Rune is literally two (or more) Runes bound together. They work as a visual of the intent of the spell. They mark a magickal beginning in the quest for a goal. Their strength (like any spell) comes from their creation and use. There is no law of three in the Northern Realms (for one because logically all evil people would be dead and therefore unable to harm anyone), in fact we often find curses like placing a Nithing Pole (a series of Runes carved with the intention of causing a curse to be laid upon someone) or the use of a carved bowl or animal hide with serious intent put upon it. Of course most who hold the Old Gods in regard, including Satanists, adhere to a core of ethics to not harm the undeserving. Alas it is only the Sons of Abraham that fall into the vile habits of kidnapping, abusing, raping and enslaving the innocent and are then, they themselves enslaved in their own minds in a never ending cycle of abuse. Best not to walk down that path my friends!

Ah but we have digressed! Back to the subject at hand…A bind rune is two to eight runes bound together for a magickal purpose or spell. The can be made for any purpose and can include runes that represent the letters of your name or other aspects about you or the person you are using them on.

Bind Runes can be made in several ways; from putting them in a Circle, Square, Rectangle or Diamond (Inguz) shape to working them in together and bridging off one another like we see in the Cross Helm or the Helm of Awe. They can then be used as jewelry for protection, put in your vehicle, made into a tattoo (permanent or with henna and worn for a smaller duration), written on a parchment, animal hide, stick or stone, then carried and put just about anywhere.

For a Primer on Runes seek out our book The Art of Divination. For the purpose of this chapter decide on your intent, choose your runes according to your intent, and then note that there are Nine Runes that have no Mirror image. These are Isa, Jera, Dagaz, Sowilo, Eihwaz, Gebo, Hagalaz, Inguz, and Nauthiz. Any one of these will therefore make a great center or start for your bind rune. Choose one that most closely aliens with your intent and start your bind rune from it.

Begin creating your bind rune, but be careful to not reverse a rune unless you are cursing someone as it will have unintended consequences. Search what you have made and try to make two other images with the runes you selected, then choose the one that suits you best.

When you are finished see if there may be any hidden runes inside. For instance Isa is a straight line and therefore hides often, but often times Gebo or Kenaz will show up as well. Make sure that these hidden runes are in line with your intent. Once you have decided on your bind rune and are satisfied, gather your materials. Of course these will depend greatly on where you desire to put your bind rune, and how long you desire it to be there. This will determine the size, for instance if on a small flat rock or a post it; while the rock will be more permanent, it won't very likely fit in your check book. So the intent of what you intend to do with your bind rune once it's made and where you intend to put it or keep it is very important.

Now you have the design set, the size determined, have decided where it will go, then it's time to decide what you are writing it with. Some prefer ink, some are burned into wood or leather and some are bound in blood. All my divination runes are both wood burnt and bound in my blood. As a woman it's not necessary to cut myself to achieve this result but it's not necessary to give a blood sacrifice to get blood either. Most of us bump our toes, get a nose bleed, or cut our fingers making dinner eventually, just have the presence of mind to then use it on that bind rune you have been sporting around! However I also have a bind rune on a wooden spoon that I use for stirring honey into my tea to open doors and bring opportunities, this rune of course, I didn't bind in blood but often eat honey with it so it's bound in my saliva.

Now it's certainly not necessary to put up an entire ritual to make a bind rune, you can if it helps you focus, but the rune will grow in power the more you think about it anyway. I like to make my bind runes (usually painted on my body) on the new moon so it grows with the moon cycle but that isn't necessary either as magick should be cast when it's needed. And when you have the uninterrupted time to put the intent into it. If you are a parent or a student or live in a house with others just grab the time when so ever you can... even if you have to do it in your vehicle to gather some uninterrupted peace!

Be sure and focus on each rune as you place it. Some like to say a spell, I urge you however to sing a chanty (2-4 line rhyming spell) in your head as the Norse and the Celts sung to their Gods and Goddesses. I have included several throughout this book for all manner of intents and purposes. Once you have your bind rune finished then put it where you will think about it. If you are binding another then it can be out of sight, but every time you look in its direction or see that person, contemplate its intent. **Here are somethings to consider when making your own Bind Runes:**

Fehu: Expedites circumstances and strengthens the power of any spell.

Thurisaz: Can be used for Self Defense as well as Destruction.

Kaunaz: Will protect whatsoever you place it on, as well as banishes any negative energies directed towards you; therefore it can be great for a Book of Spells, a Book of Shadows, a Cabinet full of valuables, etc.

Algiz: Protects and Defends; Repels danger; theft and destructive energies; banishes and diminishes all ill wishes laid against you. Makes great borders on rocks and bottles.

Berkano: Is a great rune for empaths because it protects the emotions and creates a barrier so you can remove yourself from others emotions and see the outside picture.

Wunjo: Channels and Harmonizes energies; when used with Berkano will bring a happy ending for anything you have manifested with them.

Ing: Is a Binding Rune, as it fixes and holds a desired out come into place; keeps the powers from diminishing your works, protects from your works being scattered and lost or being stolen by others. It can be used as a frame work around any other rune or can be incorporated into any design.

A Spell to Bind your Runes: This rune I wind, this spell I bind; to keep my oath, to pledge my troth, by stone and tree! By sound and spell, Now bind it well, protected I am, so nothing can, come back to me! By Lord and Lady, By Spirit and Shade, As I will it, so is it made, Now mote it be!

Knot Work: Is often also used to bind a spell or to protect it by making evil lose its tracks in a never ending design. Knot work can be incorporated on the inside or outside of any bind rune. Examples of its use would be woven into designs of Dragons, Cauldrons, Solar Crosses, Shields, Hearts, Crows and of course Thor's Hammer. The Runes are then interwoven into the design or used in a circle outside of the design.

Runic Combinations to Consider:

Healing: Algiz + Berkano + Dagaz + Tiwaz

Vehicle Protection: Algiz + Berkano or Kenaz + Raidho with Ehwaz

Partnership or Contracts: Isa + Gebo + Gebo + Ingwaz

Encourage Love: Gebo + Jera

Discover Hidden Things: Pertho + Ansuz

Open Creative Channels: Raidho + Kenaz

Conquer Learning and Tests: Laguz + Ansuz

Luck: Ansuz + Gebo, Add Fehu for Gambling.

Legal Success: Raidho + Tiwaz

Shield or Armor: Gebo + Isa

Protect Energy: Algiz + Eihwaz + Jera

Wealth: Algiz + Gebo + Fehu

As Above So Below: Ingwaz + Gebo

Success in Speaking & Writing: Laguz + Ansuz + Fehu

Success gained through revelation of hidden knowledge: Sowilo + Perthro + Kenaz with Ansuz

Protect Ancestral Property: Algiz + Fehu + Othala

To Deliver a Curse: Nauthiz + Isa + Hagalaz + Thurisaz

To Cause Storms: Hagalaz + Thurisaz

Tarot Spells: are the use of one or more Tarot Cards to enhance a spell and work very much like a bind rune but are far less permanent and so are used on short spells (like landing a job after an interview), where a bind rune is used on a spell of long or permanent duration (like protecting ancestral property). Tarot spells are therefore meant to run their course in a moon cycle or less. If the magick hasn't been buildt up enough, then they may have to be repeated. Typically you would want to use one card from the major arcana and add two from the lower arcana that support it. We have a primer in our book The Art of Divination pages 44 through 88 for your ease of use. As a quick reminder:

The Suit of Diamonds or Wands: Is used in all matters of right brain intellect, including: schooling, knowledge, ideas and inspiration.

The Suit of Hearts or Cups: Is used for all left brain intellect of art , writing and speaking as well as the manifestation of Love.

The Suit of Clubs or Swords: Is used to bring order out of chaos, to bring form out of energy and can be used to bring conflict, separation or war.

The Suit of Spades or Pentacles: Is used to bring Wealth, Money, Comfort, Business Stability and Financial Security.

Examples:

Destruction: The Tower with upside down King or Queen of Swords to represent the victim, then a card representing what you desire to destroy: like an upside down Ten of Spades for ruining an inheritance with an upside down Seven of Spades to fulfill the financial ruin. As well the Tower can be used with the King or Queen of Clubs and a reversed Two of Hearts and a reversed Seven of Hearts to separate and destroy lovers. To reverse these spells reverse the Tower Card and use the other cards upright.

For Love: Use the Lovers card with the 10 of Hearts/Cups and the 3 of Hearts/Cups. **To Break up or Separate:** Reverse all cards.

For Success: Use the Chariot card with the 8 of Clubs/Swords and the 2 of Clubs/Swords. **To Destroy:** Reverse all cards.

For Luck: Use the Wheel of Fortune with the 7 of Diamonds/Wands and the 10 of Spades/Pentacles/Coins. **To Dispel:** Reverse all cards.

For Court Cases: Use the Justice card with the 6 of Diamonds/Wands and the Ace of Diamonds/Wands. **To use Against your Opponent:** Reverse all cards.

For Renewal of Circumstances: Use the Judgement card with the 8 of Spades/Pentacles/Coins and the 6 of Spades/Pentacles/Coins. **No Reversal.**

For Needed Change: Use the Reincarnation card with the 3 of Spades/Pentacles/Coins and the Ace of Spades/Pentacles/Coins. **No Reversal.**

For Abundance: Use the Star card with the 5 of Diamonds/Wands and the 9 of Spades/Pentacles/Coins. **No Reversal.**

For Protection: Use the World card with the 9 of Hearts/Cups and either the 3 of Hearts/Cups or the Ace of Hearts/Cups. **No Reversal.**

For Real Estate: Use the Strength card with the Ace of Hearts/Cups and the 4 of Spades/Pentacles/Coins. **To Break or Disrupt a Real Estate Contract:** Reverse all cards.

Discover Treachery: Use the Moon card with the 2 of Swords/Clubs and the Ace of Swords/Clubs or the 5 of Pentacles. **No Reversal:** However be forewarned that treachery is most easily done by those closest to you and so you may well be heartbroken to discover the real culprit.

For Wealth: Use the Star card with the 6, 3 and Ace of Pentacles/Hearts. **To Destroy:** Reverse all cards.

Notes: The actual card from your beloved deck can be used by putting it on top of the spell, and keeping it a box or a honey jar to sweeten the deal. However you could go to the local library, make a copy of the card, and then write the spell on the copy. I highly suggest the latter if your intention is to bury or burn the spell.

Blessing a Key to Open up the Door to the Other World:

Herbs: Birch, Mistletoe, Yarrow, Mugwort, Elder, Basil, Sage, Violet, Fern, and Bay Leaves.

Candle: White or Purple

Materials: Bowl of Spring Water to put the herbs in, A Skeleton key for each person attending the ritual.

With this Broom I sweep this circle round (widdershins) , Evil go out so only Peace can be found!

Call your quarters, strengthen your borders, light your candles, burn some of the herbal mixture in offering. Put the rest in the bowl of spring water and with the keys and spinning a circle on the water sing:

The Spell: Upon the door between here and there we knock; Lofn lift the key, Lofn turn the lock; our dearest ancestors we come and seek, within our souls we desire to hear them speak; Hlin protect us and shield us from all harm, Frigga guide us and keep us warm; Gefion who supplies our every need, and Fulla who guards the secret mysteries; come to us now and show us the way, to the mysteries that will be revealed this day. Snotra who always knows what to do, May you and Vor show us the meanings of the secrets true. Eir heal us in every conceivable way, Sjofn show us where we can love more each day, Var hear our oath to use all wisdom well, and dear Sin close the door and end our spell!

Wield your magick, sing your songs, close the circle and give thanks and offerings to all whom you bid to come.

Keep the key either on your neck, your altar or by your bedside always.

9 ROOTS, TREES & HERBS

Hoodoo is what's called a sympathetic form of magick. That means that something that looks like, touched, can be imagined as something else, then substitutes for that something else in the spell. Witches have long used sympathetic magick as a means of working with the energy, frequencies and vibrations of the universe, and found it most effective, as we can see in William Shakespeare's play Macbeth: Fillet of a fenny snake; In the cauldron boil and bake, Eye of newt and toe of frog, Wool of bat, and tongue of dog, Adder's fork and blind-worm's sting, Lizard's leg and howlet's wing, For a charm of powerful trouble, Like a hell-broth boil and bubble!

These aren't necessarily real animals he's referring to, they are but simple plants and herbs used for their sympathetic properties that resemble these animals in some way. That way may be even that the animal referred to, was often seen to frequent the ground where the plant grows, or they peck at them, land on them, or even scrounge amoung the plants. It may be that the plant referred to somehow resembles the substance called for (blood, semen), then again say in the reference of Foxglove, being a poisonous plant that has often been used to kill people, bloody fingers may well refer to the blood on the hands of the person who picked it. In the case of Hawthorne, Bread and Cheese may refer to that it was used as a meal in the suffering times. There are many different reasons these herbs are could be considered sympathetic to the Witch who Wields them. Beginning on the next page is a list of herbs, and different plants; their sympathetic magickal names and/or uses or their magickal properties. All plants are connected and so one with the same attributes either magickally or sympathetically may be substituted for the other. This is completely different from our herbal grimoire in our book "One Pot Witchery's Stone Soup" as these plants are for use in sympathetic magick only and so their medicinal properties and actions are not noted. Again, this list is for use of Sympathetic Magick ONLY, many of the plants are highly poisonous or invasive. Great care should be taken when gathering or using. These herbs are NOT for teas, tinctures, or salves so please, unless you are completely familiar with a plants medicinal qualities and actions, Only Wield it, NEVER CONSUME IT!!!

SYMPATHETIC MAGICKAL NAMES OR USES FOR ROOTS, TREES & HERBS:

LETTER A:

Acacia: (Gum Arabic, Origin of Horus) Turns back fiends, evil doers, and causes the Eye of Ra to rest upon its seat. Protection, Psychic Powers; magickally substitutes for Aconite, Allspice, Cassia and Tobacco.

Aconite: (Wolfbane, Monk shod, Spittle of Cerberus, Poison Arrow, Flint wort, Stone herb, Woman Killer, Scorpion's Tail, Thor's Plant, Heart of a Boogity): Protection, Invisibility; magickally substitutes for Acacia, Allspice, Cassia and Tobacco. Was used to turn into a werewolf, and Calpurnius Bestia killed his wives by touching their genitals with the powder.

Adder's Tongue Fern: (Sparrow's Tongue, Snake's Tongue, Serpent's Tongue, Dog's Tooth, Trout Lily) Prevents Evil from entering the Home, Antitheft, Staves off Illness; Magickally substitutes for cowbane, woodruff and dittany of Crete.

Agaric: (Death Angel, Magic Mushroom, Red Cap, Death Cap) Can be used to bring fertility or to cause great sickness or death to fall on someone. It is associated with the season of Yule. And this is the mushroom you often see in fairy rings.

Agrimony: (Church Steeples, Stickwort, Liverwort, Harvest Lice, Fairy's Wand, Wolf's Milk) Protection and Sleep. It was said if laid under a bed that it would magickally induce sleep. Agrimony boiled in fresh milk was cited as a cure for male impotence by the Leech Book of Bald, compiled in the 9th century. A wondrous work compiled by Cild the monk that catalogs the various herbs and wort cunning and even surgeries of the Anglo Saxons of that time. It is now housed in the British Library. So this herb also sympathetically works to heal infertility in males, at least temporarily.

Ague Root: (Crow Corn, Blazing Star, Unicorn Root) used in hex breaking and uncrossing rituals to keep evil at bay.

Angelica: (Master Wort, Holy Ghost Root, Archangel Root)used for protection, , exorcism, healing and visions, removing hexes, curses or spells and enhances the aura. Ingesting it is said to cause a disgust of liquors.

Apple Tree: (Crab Apple, Wild Apple, Somerset, Johnny Appleseed) Used for cider, wines, pies, sauces and vinegar making. The star shaped core is used as a natural pentagram in rituals and magick. Carved and dried to make Apple Dolls (which can cleverly substitute as a Boogity). Considered a tree of immortality, it was fed to the Norse gods by Indunn to keep them forever young. Apple wands are used in Norse love rituals and are said to represent long life, wisdom and love. It is also said to induce prophetic dreams by sleeping under it or by putting an apple under your pillow at night. The Medieval church believed that you could give an apple to a person to cause possession (we don't know about that but we have a very effective apple cures printed in our The Art of the Boogity book!). It is considered able to heal, and bestow youth, vitality and rebirth to a person (for these benefits you must eat one nightly before going to bed). Apples are buried in churchyards and at Samhain to feed the dead. The Apple tree has links to Druids, and Shamans and is sacred to many deities including Cerridwen, and Freyja.. Apples always have a place at the Dumb Supper. Honoring the Apple Tree Man is done on January 6th by wassailing (throwing apple cider on it roots) the oldest apple tree in the orchard and shooting arrows thought the branches to ward off evil spirits as well as leaving offerings for the birds to bring a good harvest in the year to come. The Apple Tree is used for wish magick by either tying your wish to the tree or carving it into an apple. Apple cider substitutes for wine or ale in any ritual. Apples are good for healing, wishing, feeding the dead and curses.

May Apple: (Devil's apple, Wild mandrake, Witches Umbrella, Hog apple, Raccoon berry) Used to keep things hidden from prying eyes, The root when tucked under a mattress assures fertility, Hung inside a high place in the home it brings prosperity and luck. Substitutes for Mandrake.

Amaranth: (Love Lies Bleeding, Red Cockscomb, Lamb's quarter, Lady bleeding, Spleen) Healing, Protection, Invisibility, and Immortality. Used in religious ceremonies to grant supernatural powers, its flowers are put on graves and when burned the ashes produce saltpeter.

Anemone: (Wind Flower, Pasque Flower, Blood of Adonis) Brings luck, protects against evil, closes its petals when rain is approaching, and harbor the fairies at night.

Arnica: (Lamb's coat, Wolf flower) Drives away thunder storms, brings fertility to crops and will keep a spirit from leaving or entering while it is in bloom.

Asafetida: (Devils Dung, Food of the Gods) the resin of the root is used for Exorcism, Purification, Protection, dispelling disease, and repelling insects .

Avens: (Gosling Wing, Golden Star, Star of the Earth, Blessed Herb) Fends off evil spirits, venomous beasts and the plague. Made into an amulet, it is said to protect the home from Satan. Exorcism, Protection and Love.

LETTER B:

Bachelor's Buttons: (Devil's flower, Blue bottle, Hurtsickle) worn to see if your love is returned (by how quickly it fades or not). A wreath hung is said to aid your journey into the underworld and resurrect the dead.

Balmony: (Snake Head, Turtle head, Bitter herb, Chelone, Fish Mouth) used for shapeshifting, steadfastness, patience and perseverance.

Bay Laurel: (Blue Jay, Daphne's Repulsion, Apollo's Rejection) attracts romance, used for divination, predicting disaster, purification and protects the home from lightning.

Bears Breeches: (Blood from a Shoulder, Sea dock, Oyster plant, Bear's Foot) healing magick.

Belladonna: (Dwale, Enchanter's Nightshade, Death's Herb, Devil's berries, Naughty man's cherries, Bane wort, Beautiful death) Used to call Hekate and to curse or cross others, very popular in flying ointments.

Betony: (Lion's Hairs, Lamb's Ears, Bishop wort, St. Brigid's comb, Woundwort) worn as an amulet to ward off evil spirits.

Biden's: (Beggar's Tick, Black Jack, Cockhold) used by women to mask their infidelity and be able to pass of the offspring of the union as someone else's (like their husbands), also used to control a husband.

Bindweed: (Morning glory, Creeping Jenny, Possession bind, Devil's guts) any ivy type plant that climbs trees can be used for binding and creating bridges between the realms; magickally substitutes for High John the Conqueror. Don't grow it in your yard though as it takes over everything can is impossible to get rid of.

Birch Tree: (The White Lady of the Woods) It is important to note that the Changa mushroom grows on the birch tree and is considered one of the most healing mushrooms in the world. The birch heralds new beginning and is used as representative as the first rank. It is considered very protective. Brooms made of birch wood are said to drive out the spirits and are used to beat the bounds of property for protection. The Yule log as well as the Beltane fire is traditionally made of birch. Cradles made of birch protect the newborn from the Land of Sidhe (Fairy's) and from any psychic harm or evil eye that may be laid on it. A piece of birch carried in your pocket works against kidnapping as well.

Bistort: (Dragon Wort, Easter giant, Pudding grass, Red legs, Snake Weed) Bistort Leaves: (Dragon Scales)

Blackberry: (Scald head, Bramble fruit)protects against spells and curses when gathered on the new moon, also known to protect from enemies and large animals.

Black Earth: (Crocodile Dung) Used to draw things out and away.

Black Haw: (Knight's Milfoil, King's Crown, May, May Rose, Silver Bells) used to prevent cramps and miscarriages; either as a tea or a wash.

Black Cohosh Root: (Black Snake Root, Bugbane, Rattle root) Used for Protection and Strength.

Blackthorn Tree: Sacred to Morrigan, Cerridwen and Cailleach. The wood is used for walking sticks and Irish shillelaghs. The ripe Sloe berries sweetens after the first frost are then used to make Sloe Gin, and Jam. It is considered a tree of Ill Omen. It is used for left hand work and is sacred to the dark goddesses and crone aspect. Blackthorn is called the keeper of secrets, represents war, wounding and death. Wands made from it are used for curing, blasting, binding, confusion, creating boundaries, purification, embracing your dark nature, and the thorns are often used in Boogitys and to pierce the heart of a black chicken to curse someone. Black thorn can also be used for protection and the Norse Rune Thurisaz (Thorn), on them for this. In fact many bind runes have a center and branches sticking out to represent the protection of being surrounded by a thorn tree. "With Blackthorn staff I draw the bound, All malice and bane I thus confound". Magick circles are made with it at Samhain when the Morrigan and Dagda are said to mate. Wands made of Blackthorn on May day are used for divination, fertility and wishes.

Bloodroot: divide clumps at four years and harvest at six years to use for hex breaking, protecting marriage and promoting harmony. You can hang it above your door or in your pillow or under your mattress for this. Can be used instead of blood in any spell.

Blue Bells: (Ring-o-bells, Fairy flower,) used by fairy's to trap humans. If a child picks a bluebell in the woods they will never be seen again. If an adult picks one, they will wander lost forever, or at least until rescued. Anyone wearing a wreath of them is compelled to speak the truth, used to win the heart of whom you desire, prevents nightmares and comforts the mourning.

Bluets: (Jacob's Staff, Innocence, Quaker Ladies) used to bring contentment to a household.

Borage: (Star Flower, Mouse ear, Lungwort, Bee Bread)used to calm the heart, purge melancholy, pacify lunatics, promote cheer and merriment.

Brier Hips: (Witches Briar, Rose hips, Briar Rose, Dog Rose) crack open to create an itching powder for use in hoodoo, or to put in peoples clothes or on poppets.

Buckthorn: (Bone of an Ibis, Buffalo berry, Autumn Olive) the wood is used to produce charcoal, the bark when mixed with iron makes a black ink.

Bugle Weed: (Wolf Foot, Nose bleed, Gypsy wort) used for dissolving disease, problems, and bad situations.

Bugloss: (Ox Tongue) protection, healing and to find and curse the snakes in the grass (false friends)

Burdock: (Beggar's Buttons, Frog's Foot, Fox's Clote, Love Leaves, Bird's Eye) used for finding out if a love sticks to you or will fall away. Carried in a red flannel bag to prevent rheumatism.

Butchers Broom: Irish Tops, Jew's Myrtle, Knee Holly) Is used to make brooms to clean butcher blocks and to deter rodents from meat hanging to cure. In sympathetic magick it is used to repel, especially to repel unwanted suitors, stalkers or anyone who won't leave you alone.

Bulbous buttercup: (Frog's Foot, Toe of Frog, From the Belly)as a game children put them under others chins to see if that person likes butter, In magick it is used to reflect curses back to the sender.

LETTER C:

Calamus: (Sweet Flag, Sweet Cane or Grass Myrtle) used to bind, as a stimulant for spells or and as an hallucinogen.

Calamint: (Lizard, Wild Basil) takes away melancholy, brings in gladness and is worn by pregnant woman to aid the birthing process.

Canadian Snake Root: (Cat's Foot, Canadian Wild Ginger) the roots are steeped in alcohol to make perfume. Can substitute for ginger in a spell but never medicinally as it can be poisonous.

Cannabis: (Bhang, Sacred Grass, Ganja, Charas, Pantagruelian)Used in magick and health for healing, bringing calm to anger, getting past emotional hurt, overcoming PTSD, scrying, and prior to astral projection.

Carob: (Jupiter's Foot, John's Bread) protection and health.

Carolina Reaper: (The Grim Reaper) dried it is used in sympathetic magick as a boogity heart. We used to use a dried ghost pepper, but this works even better for the burn! Also makes a very excellent hot foot powder! But be careful not to rub your eyes while making and to wash your hands thoroughly after using!

Cat Nip: (Cat) Cat magick, love, beauty and happiness.

Cedar: (Blood of Kronos, Ladies Meat) Sacred to the Goddess and to Baal (psalm 29 was originally written for Baal), symbolizes the vagina or gate to the womb, and is used to call upon the ancestors.

Celandine: (Devil's Milk) used to bring clarity to a situation, sharpen the sight and dispel the slimy things.

Chamomile: (Blood of Hestia, From the Loins, Gazel's Hooves, Plant Doctor) Wards off disease, burned brings wealth, used as a wash for your hands brings luck and success in gambling, banishes negative spirits, induces sleep. Best picked on a Sunday when the sun or moon is in Leo. When planted next to any other plant will bring health to your garden.

Cherry Tree Gum: (Brains, Hag berry, Hackle berry, Witch's Tree) Burned for Love, Exorcism and Divination.

Chick Weed: (Star Weed) promote fidelity, attract Love. Spirituality, success, healing, power, psychic powers, lust, protection, money and love.

Chinese Sumac: (Toad, Nut gall, Indian salt-refers to the powder on the berries, Sacred Pipe) leaves can be mixed with tobacco for sacred smoke.

White Cinnamon: (White Wood) Burned at funerals, used for Spirituality, Mummification, Blessing, Money, Success, Healing, Power, Psychic Powers, Lust Protection and Love.

Cinquefoil: (Five Finger Grass, Five Fingers, Felon Herb, Tormentil, Flesh and Blood) used in spells for Love, Money and Success, in mixtures of Van Van, and as a protection bath to keep evil far away.

Clary Sage: (Clear-Eye, eye of Christ) Used in wine or beer recipes to increase intoxification, to clear melancholy, as an aphrodisiac, and to calm the nerves.

Cleavers: (Goose Grass: Everlasting Friendship, :Love Man, Robin Run In The Grass, Sweet Hearts) used as a bath to be successful in love, a tonic produces milk in mothers, also used as a dye to turn bones red.

Clover: (Semen of Helios, Semen of Aries, Hare's Foot, Rabbit's Foot, Serpent's Tongue) attracts money and prosperity, chases out evil and ghosts, breaks curses, protects from the evil eye, allows one to see and interact with the other world, protects the body of the traveler who walks between the worlds, used as tobacco, incense and a ritual offering.

Club Moss: (Wolf Claw, Druid's Hand, Stag Horn, Tears of a Baboon) actually a ground creeping fern and not a moss; the spore dust can be added to stretch any magickal powder or tossed into a fire to produce a bright flash.

Cockscomb: (Yellow Rattle) Silliness, Affection, Pretension and Singularity.

Coeloglossum: (Frog Orchid, Hollow Tongue, Hounds Tongue) used in fertility spells, spells for sexual reproduction and spells to stop gossip,

Colt's Foot: (Bull's Foot, Ass's Foot, Foal's Foot, Horse Hoof, Horse's Tongue) used in love, peace and money spells, burned for divination, and healing.

Comfrey: (Ear of an Ass, Soapwort, Knit bone and Bone set) Protection in traveling, protection against theft, vehicle protection to keep a lover faithful, healing, joining things back together and as a money wash for gambling'

Couch Grass: (Dog grass) roots are eaten by sick dogs, magickally expels sickness and disease, also for exorcism of spirits.

Cowage Plant: (Donkey's Eye) the pods are used for cursing (to cause itches and stings) and vines for bindings.

Cowslip: (Fairy Cup, Herb peter, Key of Heaven) used in washes to promote peace in a household, also used to promote sleep.

Crawley Root: (Chicken Toe, Scaly Dragon's Claw) used for crossroads magick, making or breaking contracts.

Cynosurus: (Dog's Tail, Bennets)useful to get someone to follow you.

LETTER D:

Daisy: (Eyes, Eye of the Star, Eye of the Day, Fairy Smoke, White Ox eye, Dutch-curse) Used in the children's rhymes He/she loves me, She/he loves me not and This year, Next Year, Sometime, Never when plucking the flowers to see when you will marry. Used for Midsummer festivities, to get a lover to return, wards off lightning, keeps children safe from fairies, and is used for Lust and Luck and chasing away Sorrow.

Dandelion: (Priest's Crown, Rabbit's Foot, Pig's Snout, Swine Snout, Lion's Teeth, Urine, Farmer's Clock and Weather Watch) Bow on the seeds of a dandelion; if you can blow all the seeds off with one blow then you are loved with a passionate love; if some seeds remain then your lover has reservations and if a lot of seeds remain then your lover is false. Its flowers always open at 5 am and close at 8pm and so can be used as an outdoors clock. The balls will close up if wet weather is approaching. Used for wish magick by making a wish and blowing it out to the universe, Lust, Luck, Divination, as a Psychic tea and for Calling Sprits. The Root summons chthonic spirits. The leaves summon nature spirits and spirits of the middle realm. The seeds and flowers summon the spirits of the sky; the Gods and the Goddesses as well as enhance divinations and psychic abilities when brewed into a tea. The powder can be smoked, the flowers can be fried or made into wine, and the root can be made into coffee or used as a fetish.

Datura: (Devil's Apple, Jimson Weed, Mad Hatter, Moon Flower, Witch's Thimble) used to commune with the spirit world, cause madness in a person, give a person nightmares, make them confess their sins, (we use the roots for Boogity Brains), can be chewed to discover a thief (but also produces hallucinations for up to two weeks, madness and sometimes death) and so is better sprinkled as a powder on the place where the theft occurred for that purposes. All parts are highly poisonous.

Death Cap Mushroom: (Skull, Phallus, Destroying Angel) It is the most poisonous of all toadstools and their poison is not reduced by cooking, freezing or drying them. In fact it is responsible for most of all mushroom deaths worldwide as it closely resembles edible mushrooms. It is said that less than half of one will kill an adult and if you do survive that your liver will be destroyed. By the time symptoms appear (2-3 days after ingestion) your internal organs have suffered irreparable damage. Death occurs between 6-16 days after ingestion. There is no antidote. Clearly this mushroom should only be used in sympathetic magick and not touched without gloves. Sympathetically it substitutes as the person you desire to grant an excruciating death to in a coffin spell.

Devil's Shoestring: (Hobble bush, Cramp Bark, Black Haw, Crossroads Root or Root of the Crossroads) used to trip up the devil, success spells for business, career, employment, raises, protection, gambling spells, protect against gossip and crossed conditions, and protect against hot footing.

Dill: (Semen of Hephaistos, Semen of Hermes, Hare's Beard, Tree of Heaven, Hairs of a Baboon, Tears of a Baboon, Meetinghouse seeds)Protection, Happiness Good Fortune, Prosperity, Money, Lust and Luck. Can be added to Bridal bouquets or bouquets of flowers brought into a new house.

Dittany of Crete: (Joy of the Mountains, Burning Bush) heals open wounds, used as a perfume and flavoring for liquors, used as an aphrodisiac, and in love magick.

Dodder: (Devil's Guts, Witch's Hair, Love Vine, Cuscuta, Strangle tare, Fire Weed, Devils Saffron) used in sympathetic magick to bind or choke out an opponent. Substitutes for saffron.

Dragon's Blood Resin: (Sandre de Grado, Dracaena, Daemonorops) used as an incense for cleansing, in the creation of mojo hands for love or money, removes negative energies and spirits and is very useful as an ink as well. Also very useful in healing magick and protection for rituals.

LETTER E:

Elder or Elm Gum: the gum produced from a tree being sieged by bark beetles, used in sympathetic magick as a slow ongoing curse that won't let go of the victim and eventually causes them to wither away. May also be used to extend the curse to family members or neighbors.

Elder: (Old Lady, Old Girl, Old Woman) Is used for Jams, jellies, medicinal syrups and wine (pick the berries on midsummer eve for a magickal feast!). An Elder must not be cut down without first saying: Old Woman give me some of thy wood, and I will give you some of mine when I grow into a tree. (an Elder, get it, like a Grandma). Precious to the Goddess, it was thought that the Elder woman lived in its trunk. Witches were thought to use Elder branches as horses. The crooked bent Elder was often thought to be a Witch. Burning Elder logs is said to bring the devil into the house. The juice is used upon the eyes to see fairies and witches. They are said to be the home of elves. The Elder is considered very protective and solar crosses made of Elder are used to protect homes, barns and people.

Elecampane: (Enchanter's Plant, Horse Heal, Elf Wort, Tears of Troy, Devils Bit) Binds Love, used by the Celts in a bath to Protect against evil magick with Rue, Nettle, Verbena, Yarrow, Mugwort, Wood Betony, Celandine, and White Clover. Also used to enhance Psychic Powers. Burned it is Furnitory and known as Earth Smoke, can also be used as a substitute for Wax Dolls.

Elder Sap: (Blood, Devil's Spit) Keeps evil spirits out, protects against disease, and used in beauty baths and potions.

Eye Bright: (Eyes, Graces) used for healing of the eyes, and spells for second sight or the use of familiars.

Evening Primrose: (Donkey's Herb, Fever Plant, War Poison, German Rampion) It is used for successful hunting by scrubbing your clothes with it to mask your scent, therefore in sympathetic magick it imparts a degree of invisibility when laydown track magick.

LETTER F:

False Unicorn Root: (Unicorn's Horn, Blazing Star, Fairy Wand) used to prevent miscarriage and treat ovarian cysts, sympathetic magickal uses include healing, as a wash for new mothers, as well as averting danger and evil.

Fern: (Skin of Man); the unexpanded frond from a male fern (Hair) used in invisibility magick or to hide treasure and other valuables. Also considered lucky and to bring prosperity and fertility to a household.

Feverwort: (Centaury, Filwort) used to call Chiron, bring good luck, in health spells with dog wood and willow bark to aid in breaking fevers, and it I used to ward away evil spirits.

Figwort: (Crowdy Kit, Thousand Blessings, Thousand Virtues) dissolves clotted and congealed blood in bumps and bruises; used magickally to open roadways and passages, protect from disease and the evil eye. Also used in washes to bring blessings into a home.

Flea Bane: (Semen of Horus, Semen of Hephaistos, Old Man in the Spring) used as an insect repellant, kept as sachets in beds. Sympathetic magick is used to repel evil and protect.

Foxglove: (Fat from a Head, Lady's Mantle, Bloody Fingers, Fairy Fingers, Fairy Gloves, Witches Bells, Goblin's Glove) used in fairy magick, in fertility magick, is used to warn others of coming evil, can break fairy enchantments and is highly poisonous.

Fringe Tree: (Ox's Eye, Old Man's Beard, Snow Drop) used in healing magick, especially for headaches.

LETTER G:

Galangal (Low John, Chewing John, Little John) : Curse Breaking, Passion, Health, Exorcism, Protection, Power. Money and Court cases.

Garlic: (An Eagle, Poor Man's Treacle, Satan's Foot) Protection from demons, Summons Hekate, Strength, Healing, Lust and Antitheft, Oath taking, Wards against evil spirits (causing them to lose their way) and disease (garlic braids are often hung in kitchens in the winter for this purpose). Also said to ward off the evil eye, werewolves and vampires and were hung in windows for this purpose. Also binds heavy metals and excretes them.

Spotted Geranium: (Cranesbill, Crow's Foot) roots can be used to tan hides, used to counter-act a love spell, attract happiness and prosperity, encourage conceptions and well as the successful birth and well-being of the child.

Geranium: (Dove's Foot, Old Maid's Nightcap, Chocolate Flower, Crow Foot, Shame Face) Happiness, Prosperity, Fertility, Health, Love and Protection. They are also used as Talismans and the color of the flowers or smell of the leaves can substitute in sympathetic magick for any number of things (pepper, roses etc.).

Germander Speedwell:(Bird's Eye, Eye of Newt, Mother Die) Used in sympathetic magick in curses and death spells. Often used by the other woman, so as to replace her as the new wife and stepmother.

Ginseng: (Man Root, Tarter Root) can be used as a poppet for health, is said to eliminate evil chi, and prevent disease.

 Golden Seal: (Eyes, Eye Root, Yellow Root) Guardian and Healer, providing strength and protection to those who possess it. Wards off evil and brings good luck. It is often put into a white flannel bag with angelica root and other healing herbs, and blessed with oil and then sewn into the mattress to help alleviate the pain and suffering of chronic pain, disease or acute illness.

Gravel Root: (Queen of the Meadow Root, Joe Pye weed) brings good luck to lovers and gamblers alike.

LETTER H:

Hart's Tongue Fern: (Holy Herb, Deer Tongue, God's Hair, Hind's Tongue) Used to dispel things as it will die in its third year of growth it its spores don't reseed it. Good for planting spells under that you want to go away or die like that creepy uncle or family friend everyone trusts but you.

Hawthorne: (Bread and Cheese, Hawthorn, Fairy Thorn, Corpse Blossom, The May) Considered a blessing or a curse depending on when it is picked. By some it is the unluckiest of all plants, in which bringing it into a house is said to cause illness, financial loss or death. The leaves can be eaten and are referred to as bread and cheese. The blossoms and berries are made into wine and jams. The blossoms do however smell like a rotting corpse and for this reason they are used in sympathetic magick I coffin spells. Be careful in gathering though as the Fae have a liking for stealing anyone away brave enough to try. The custom of bringing in the May was the gathering of branches from the blossoming Hawthorne tree in which many legends expound. An example being: The fair maid who, the first of May; goes into the fields at break of day, and washes in dew from the Hawthorne tree, will ever after, handsome be! In Greece it was used as a marriage torch and brides wore a crown of it in their hair. Witches were said to make their brooms from it as referred to in this rhyme: Hawthorne bloom and Elder flowers, will fill a house with evil powers; therefore in sympathetic magick just giving it in a bouquet to anyone after the month of May but before the month of December will bring evil and bad luck to their household.

Hawk Weed: (Mouse's Tail, Devil's Paintbrush, Rattlesnake Weed, The King Devil, Mouse's Ear) Very invasive, often destroying other plants and is poisonous, therefore used in domination, control and cursing.

Hazel: Used for dowsing water sources. Hazel nuts and Hazel mead is said to bring inspiration and knowledge (as it is psychotropic). It is considered the Tree of Knowledge and is sacred to Thor. It is considered an entrance into the other realm. The nuts associated with fertility and a great showing of them in spring means lots of babes to be born. Hazel nuts are roasted at Samhain and if two people throw theirs in the fire together they could tell where the relationship was bound in the coming year (by whether the nuts stayed together or split apart in the roasting), It is used for protection from lightning, in travel, against disease and the evil eye. Hazel nuts carried are said to ward off Rheumatism. Wands and staffs are said to be the key that opens the door to the fairy realm.

Heliotrope: (Clytie, Cherry Pie)Gathered in August the plant is supposed to amplify any spell done with it back to you so it is good to do prosperity and love spells with it at this time. However never use it for bane, because it will return it to you as well. It can be burned for banishing. Plant near beehives as they come up early to feed the bees in spring.

White/Black Hellebore: (Semen of Herakles, Semen of Helios, Lenten Rose) Means "To Injure" and is highly poisonous. It is used for banishing, exorcism, protection, invisibility, increasing intellect, healing the emotions and summoning demons.

Hemp Agrimony: (Holy Rope) grows near water and is used as a poultice to draw out poisons and relieve boils. Used in healing magick.

Hen Bane: (Devils Eye, Witch Plants) is believed to attract rain, raise storms, blight crops and livestock. Leaves are used for brewing beer, seeds are used for stunning chickens for slaughter. It is burned for funerals, prophecy, rituals of necromancy and summoning spirits. Henbane Pilsner 20 liters of water 1 liter of malt 1/2 liter honey 40 grams of dried henbane leaves, yeast for beer (amount depends on the product) Find a container which is large enough to hold all the ingredients. Cook the henbane in water for 5 to 10 minutes. Meanwhile dissolve the malt in a couple of liters of water, dissolve the honey into it and add the henbane leaf-water. Then add the yeast. It might be useful to add a little bit more yeast than recommended because the tropane-alkaloids affect the yeast. Don't seal the container as it may explode. The brew should start fermenting after a day or so and the fermentation should be finished after 4 or 5 days. The beer is now ready for drinking. You can also bottle it, in which case you can add a few drops of honey to each bottle and let it ferment for another week or two. Serve preferably chilled. Store as normal beer.

Holly: (Bat's Wings, Tree of Hope, Renewal) One of the Vines that are Sacred to the Druids. Holly reigns over the dark season, and signifies growth, fertility and its red berries, blood. Indeed in its biannual fight for dominance with the Oak King, The Holly King reigns over the Yule festivities. A prickly edged one represents a male, a smooth leafed one, a female and the one brought in on Christmas Eve, determined whole ruled the home in the year to come. If however it was barren (no berries) it signified infertility of herd and field, and could beacon death as well. There are various legends about when to bring the holly down or whether to burn it or keep it for luck, however in most places burning the holy meant the death of winter and so it was often burnt at springtime to represent the suns return. Holly was, like Rowan, said to keep evil at bay and so a stout stick was considered protective for night walking. Holly was also put over doorways, and made into steps to protect from witches. A holly hedge may be planted near a door for the same reason. Holly wands are used for divination, dreams and protection.

Honeysuckle: (Goat's Leaf, Bond of Love, Devoted Love, Fidelity) Have you ever sucked the end of a honeysuckle as a child? It is very invasive and can be made into rope. It is said to be a living symbol of steadfastness and love. Some say bringing a honeysuckle vine into your home will bring a wedding to follow within a year, others say its bad luck because it bewitches the females of the household into positions in which would cause them to need marriage! Honey suckle is used to bind lovers in spells. It attracts bees, butterflies and hummingbirds and can be used to protect against erosion (but must be frequently cut back). Honeysuckle vines are hung on barns to prevent cattle from being bewitched.

Hops: (Nightingale) A relative of Stinging Nettle and Cannabis, they are used for Healing and Sleep. Its use allowed you to produce more beer from less malt, preserve weaker beers so they keep longer, and aid in clarification and head retention. Hops hung in a house bring luck, hung on the bed post or put in the pillow bring sleep. Hops Tea is good for cleansing the blood and as a muscle relaxant. Used in Dream spells and to bring calm to a household.

Houseleek: (From the Loins, Thunder Plant, Joy of the Mountain, Semen of Ares, Semen of Ammon, Thor's Beard, Hens and Chicks) Exorcism, Healing, Banishing. Houseleek juice banishes warts, boils, shingles, ear ache, acne, and Impetigo. It is grown on roof tops to avoid lightning strikes, and keep witches from landing there.

Horse Tail: (Paddock Pipes, Puzzle Grass, Pewter Wort) Used in fertility mixes and mojos and placed in the bedroom. Can be used to clean metal. Also used to stop bleeding wounds externally and internally.

Horehound: (Bull's Blood, Seed of Horus, Eye of the Star, Eye Root, Shepherd's Heart)Used as an antidote for vegetable poisons. In sympathetic magick it is used for healing and exorcism.

Hydrangea: (Seven Barks, Frigidity, Heartlessness, Boastfulness) A single woman must never grow hydrangea near her house or she will never wed. Hydrangea stands for friendship, devotion and understanding, therefore it is a good peace plant for friends in which to make up. It is also said to have the ability to break curses and love spells, especially love spells put on you without your knowledge.

LETTER I:

Indian Paintbrush: (Snake's Friend, Prairie Fire, Painted Lady)Is most used as a love charm or a charm to not get pregnant. Since it is a semi parasitic plant, it can be used as a Watcher's plant over someone to keep an eye on them.

Indian Pipe: (Fairies' Finger, Fairy Smoke, Corpse Plant, Death Plant) The plant grows white on the bowels of rotting trees and once its picked or its cycle ends, then it turns black as death. It is said to be able to heal the broken heart of those mourning the loss of a loved one.

English Ivy: (Cat's Foot, Bind Wood, Love Stone, Poet's Crown) A Vine Sacred to the Druids and very invasive, often taking over areas and destroying native plants. The black berries represent night and in some places Ivy played the Queen to Holly's King. It is used to bind things together. Hung with Holly it brings peace to a household. It is considered a promise of friendship and fidelity and worn or carried by brides to bring fertility and luck in marriage. Houses and Churches are often decorated with it at Yule. Holly is a shelter and food for bird and other animals in the winter. English Ivy, English Holly, and English Laurel have all been proven useful in cancer treatment and so make a great healing wash or floor sweep to combine with treatment. It is grown around the fence as a protector, and guards against negativity and disaster. Ivy wands are used for nature and fertility rites.

LETTER J:

Chewing John: (Galangal Root) used for curse breaking, passion, protection, health and money spells. Chew the root, swallow the juice and spit the cud on the floor before the judge enters to have the judgement go in your favor.

John the Conqueror: (High John or Ipomoea Purga root, Prince John) A Prince, John was sold into slavery and never had his spirit broken. He became a legend as a trickster in evading his masters and went back to Africa, but not before bestowing his magick on this root.

Dixie John: (Trillium, Wake Robin or Beth Root, John Henry) A sacred female root used to facilitate child birth or treat other female problems. Often boiled to make a love potion, then dropped in the food of the man you desired. Also see Southern John, and Low John.

High John: (John the Conqueror, Ipomoea Jalapa root, Prince John) Used for Success, Money, Luck, Prosperity, Manifestation, Drawing, Attraction, Gambling and Love.

Little John: (Galangal Root) St. Hildegard of Bingen's Herb was used extensively in the 11th century to heal countless evil humors. She herself wrote down many of the Wise Woman cures of the time and so to her we owe a great debt of gratitude that their healing magick still survives. For use in healing magick and to ward off evil.

Low John (Trillium or Beth Root, John Henry) Is carried for assistance with family matters, to bring luck or love, to enhance solidify the bonds of marriage and enhance sex, and is used to break up affairs. See Dixie John and Southern John.

Southern John: (Trillium or Beth Root, John Henry) It is said if you pick one it will rain for the sky will mourn its death. Indeed it will turn brown and die quite quickly. It takes 7 years to establish itself and should only be used in extreme circumstances and never picked from the wild. Although considered a lucky root, sympathetically it's used to put a quick and final end to a relationship. Also see Low John and Dixie John.

St. John's Wort: (St John the Baptist, Devil's Scourge, Demon's Scourge, Demon's Curse, Grace of God, Ears of a Goat, Witches Herb) The herb is gathered in August then the flowers are crushed so they bleed red and added to oil for use an anointing oil. Flowers brought in on Midsummer, are hung for protection against lightning, invasion by evil spirits, illness, disease, fire and to divine longevity (the last is hung over every ones bed to see who will die first.) If stuffed in your pillow it is said St. John will come in the night and bless you. The tea is used as a cure against insanity. It is used in spells for Health, Power, Protection, Strength, Divination and Happiness. St. John's Wort is often hung above door and tucked under mattresses to protect from ghosts, dark fairies, malevolent spirits and to protect you from curses. It makes and excellent sweep and wash. Holy water is made with it by adding the herb and salt to spring water and then chanting: around and round; in and throughout, all about; the good comes in, and the ill speeds out!

Judas's Ear: (Wood ear, Jelly ear, John's Beard) Mushroom found on the roots of the Elder tree or on fallen logs that used in hot and sour soup; used in sympathetic magick to hunt down a betrayer, and send to them their just due.

LETTER K:

Kansui Root: (Wolf's Milk) The root is gathered in late autumn or early spring, the bark is peeled off, it is then dried in the sun and set in vinegar. It is then taken with Rhubarb for fluid retention in the chest. Sympathetic magick the root is used for the heart on a Healing poppet.

Knotweed Grass: (Squirrel's Ear, Beggar weed, Bird's Tongue, Red Robin. Monkey weed, Tiger staff) Invasive as it drive out native species, in fact it is so invasive that a lender will not give a loan for any property that it resides on. For this reason, in sympathetic magick is used to drive people out or get them to move, much like a hot foot.

Knot Wood: (Burl) a growth that appears on a variety of species of trees, when that tree is stressed in some way. Exceedingly beautiful, burl wood is highly prized and can be quite expensive. In sympathetic magick, a small piece or the sawdust can be used to heal a terrible circumstance or occurrence that has happened.

LETTER L:

Lady's Mantle: (Bear's Foot, Lion's Foot, Nine Hooks) Used for inflamed or bleeding wounds, or heavy menstruation. It is said that if you gather the dew drops from its leaves in May, naked and alone, it will grant you everlasting beauty. In sympathetic magick it is used as a face wash or in a bath, to bring beauty.

Lavender: (Elf Leaf) Used to counteract the evil eye, stuffed under your pillow to bring dreams of your true love, or to bestow courage when proposing marriage, ensure marital passion, attract customers (for prostitutes), protect against cruelty and violence, and used with rosemary to preserve virtue. A health cordial is made by steeping it in brandy with rosemary, cinnamon, nutmeg, and red sandalwood. The smell of it is said to tame tigers. It is boiled with rosemary, sage and eucalyptus to kill sickness and disease in the air. It is also used this way as a wash or with vinegar to clean the area (bed, floor, sheets, etc.) that a sick person has been in. The scent of Lavender with Pumpkin is considered Bewitching. An incense of lavender, basil, lemon balm, thyme, frankincense and rue can be burned for protection, peace and safety. It can also be made into a water or oil for the same reason.

Licorice Root: (Sweet Root) Used to Compel, Influence or Dominate someone by binding their picture to the root with either a red or black string, tell the root exactly what you want to happen (like get a job, keep working, etc.) and then put it under their bed or dresser. It is also used as a Binder in Love, Lust and Fidelity spells. You can add it to a tea mixture (like chai) and the person to whom you give it, won't be able to get you off their mind. Pieces can be added to Pillows with 13 pieces of Balm of Gilead to ensure their love for a year.

Lovage: (Love Parsley) Can be used in a love potion with angelica and spikenel, or with spikenard for a perfume for attracting love. It can be added to baths with oatmeal to treat skin problems and the root can be chewed to keep you awake on long drives.

Lupine: (Blood from a Head, Werewolf, Of Wolves) lupine is poisonous and is used to reestablish vegetation to burn areas because it fixes nitrogen into the soil. For sympathetic magick it is used to bring the curse of madness to someone.

LETTER M:

Maiden hair Fern: (Mother's Heart, Hair of Venus) It is considered magickal because you can put it under water and it will shimmer, then pull it out and it will come up dry because water does not cling to it. It is therefore used as a hair wash to make the hair shiny.

Magnolia: (Cucumber Tree) These have existed since the dinosaurs and are the oldest flowering plants in the world. It is associated with St. Brighid's day or Candlemas. It is used to bring a long lasting love.

Mandrake Root: (Hand of Glory, Charm of Prometheus, Duck's Foot, Dead Man's Ash) For the Hand of Glory part, Mandrake powder blown and breathed in or drank by a victim will render them completely motionless and with no control of their own mind (this is why it makes such good Zombie Powder, as well as Command and Compel, Bend Over etc.). It can easily be worked into a candle holder and used with the ancient charm "Now open, Lock! To the Dead Man's knock! Fly, bolt, bar and band! Nor move, nor swerve, joint, muscle or nerve, at the Spell of the Dead Man's Hand! Sleep, all who sleep – Wake, all who wake! But be as the dead for the Dead Man's Sake!" – Ingoldsby Legends. On the other side of the coin, Prometheus was said to have been tortured by Zeus for giving Knowledge and Wisdom to mankind. During this torture, his drops of blood are said to have created the mandrake. For this reason great magick is equated to it, and great care taken when uprooting it. It is said that one must first purify themselves by bathing in the waters of seven streams. Then invoking Hecate (to whom this root is precious), by singing or chanting the charm 7 times: "Hekate Einodia, Trioditis, lovely dame, of earthly, watery & celestial fame, Sepulchral, in a saffron veil, arrayed, pleased with dark ghosts that wander through the shade; Perseis, solitary goddess, hail; The world's key bearer, never doomed to fail; I stags rejoicing, huntress, nightly seen, and drawn by bulls, unconquerable queen; Leader, Nymphe, nurse, on the mountains wandering, hear the supplicants who with holy rites thy power revere, and to the herdsman with a favoring mind draw near!" – Orphic Hymn to Hecate (2-3rd century BC). After which the root is taken and kept closed in a box. Then to consecrate it: dress yourself in dark clothing, repeat the charm 7 more times, make a small hole in the ground, (if not done at a crossroads then add crossroads dirt), give a blood sacrifice of any sort (I prefer Moon Blood but any blood from a couple drops of your own to that which was gleaned from last night's steak or lamb will do), then pour a cup of honey or put a honey soaked cake of shortbread into the pit as an offering. Sing or Chant "Moon, shine brightly; softly will I sing for you goddess – and for Hecate in the underworld, the dogs tremble before her when she comes over the graves in the dark blood. I welcome you Hecate, the grim one, stay by me until the end. Make this magickal substance as effective as that of Circe, of Medea, and of the blond Perimede." – Theocritus' 3rd century poetry. Now cover the pit and walk away without looking back. In fact it is good to throw salt in your tracks and sing nonsense for a spell. Now you may press the juice, make the powders or use as needed.

Marguerite: (Queen's Delight, Pearl, Paris Daisy) good for spells for loyal love, beauty, as well as the pure and innocent first romance.

Marjoram: (Jupiter's Staff, Joy of the Mountain) Used for Good Luck, Protection, Love, Health, Happiness, Money. If found on a grave it is said that the departed have found happiness and peace. If worn by a couple on their wedding day (woven into crowns or garlands) it is said to bring love, honor and happiness to their marriage. As a sweep it is used to sweeten the air of a stuffy household and bring happiness to it.

Marigold: (Bull's Eyes, Flower of Death) Used to dispel grief after a terrible loss of an untimely death and to honor the dead. They are also planted in gardens to keep pests at bay. **Calendula:** (Pot Marigold) Is used for Wishes, Anti-Theft, Protection, Consecration, Healing and Divination.

Marshmallow: (Althea Root, Cheeses, Sweet Weed, Mortification Root) an ointment made from the roots is said to protect you from getting burned, and grant you the ability to cast out demons. It attracts benevolent spirits and grounds them to our realm for better communication. Keep a jar on your altar or tuck it into a skull, spirit house, spirit vessel, or medicine bundle. Burnt it is a powerful exorcism herb used to banish spirits, prevent possession and protect you from curses. You can smoke the dried leaves and make an oil from them as well for you to use before doing spirit work.

Meadowsweet: (Queen of the Meadow, Bridewort) Used by the Druids for flavoring mead, used a spring floor sweep to take away stale orders, or to encourage suitors to court a young maiden. It is also used as a grave flower for the young or unmarried.

Mistletoe: (Golden Bough, Holy Wood, All Heal) Note English Mistletoe is different that American Mistletoe and the American variety is very poisonous and the English one is medicinal : NEVER MIX THEM UP! Guards against lightning, fires, disease, misfortune and having the fairy steal a newborn and return a changeling. It is used as a fertility charm. Wands and poppets made of mistletoe are used for healing.

Molucca Bean: (Fairy's Eggs, Nicker nuts, Sea Beans) They are grown in the Caribbean but often travel great distances and land on the sea shore of several countries. For this reason they are used as a good luck talisman for safe travel (especially across water) and to prevent drowning. They are also said to banish bad luck and to ease child birth.

Moss: (Bat's Wool, Wolf's Claw) There are all types of moss, all are considered lucky and are used to bring money or love. **Irish Moss:** is not a moss, it's a seaweed. It is used to bring good luck and safety during a long journey. It is used as a sweep to bring money and prosperity to a household.

Mother Wort: (Lion's tail, Heart wort) It is used to infuse waters for longevity, soothe anxiety, depression and melancholy; and to revel a secret loves identity.

Mugwort: (Five Fingers, Felon Herb, Witches Herb, Old Man, St. John's Plant) Strength, Psychic Powers, Protection, Prophetic Dreams, Healing and Astral Projection.

Mulberry Tree: (Blood of a Goose, Silkworm)It is used in pies, teas, jams, jellies and desserts. In sympathetic magick it is used to bring forbidden love.

Mullein: (Candlewick Plant, Corpse Candles, Cuddy's Lungs, King's Crown, Hawk's Heart, False Graveyard Dust, Hag's Taper, Jupiter's Staff) Is used for Courage, Protection, Health, Love, Divination and Exorcism.

Mustard Seed: (Eye of the Day, Eye of Newt) is used for Fertility, Protection from demons and aids Mental Powers. **Black Mustard Seed:** is considered to give the opposite effects and is therefore used for curses.

LETTER N:

Nettle: (Weasel Snout) Nettle Beer is used to cleanse the blood and treat old age aches and pains. Nettles can be carried for protection or hung, they are said to be a cure for male infertility and are an easement of female menopause. Plucking one by the roots and reciting the names of the sick, is said to cure them. They are sacred to the trickster and may be used in defensive magick.

Nightshade: (Dwale i.e. Trickery, Deception, Delusion) See Belladonna

LETTER O:

Oak: (Tanner's Bark)A tree sacred to Druids and considered the Tree of Life, strength, abundance, endurance and sacrifice. The tree is considered an entry way to wisdom and the other world. Oak groves are considered sacred to Brighid. Flour can be made from the acorn, as well as acorns can be fed to cows as fodder. Rubbing an Oak with your left hand on Midsummers day keeps you healthy all year. To get rid of a toothache, take a new iron nail, puncture the gum by the tooth that bleeds with it and pound it into an oak tree. Lightning struck Oak is often carried as a talisman for protection. Planting an Oak in your yard of your residence is said to provide protection of your family and the ongoing inheritance of the land and its riches for generations to come.

Olive: (Oliver, Athena's Oil) Healing, Peace, Fertility, Potency, Protection, Lust. The oil is often used as a carrier oil to make other oils and salves and has been used since the Greeks first cultivated it as an anointing oil. It is called the Cycle of life because it is used in every ceremony from birth, to marriage, to death. It is considered sacred in many cultures and it's purity has been questioned as of late as many foreign producers cut it with canola oil to stretch profits out of it. An excellent alternative is Grapeseed oil.

Orris Root: (Love Root) The root is used for love and attraction in charms and amulets. The root is also used to flavor gin. The powdered root is burned to ward off evil spirits and to help the dead on their way to the land of the blessed. Cosmetically it is used in face powders and perfumes. Please note that the root must be dried for 5 years before use.

LETTER P:

Pansy: (Love in Idleness, Hearts ease, Call Me to You) Love, Rain Magick and Divination. In love divination you are to pick a pansy, pluck one of the upper petals; then if the petal has four veins then there is hope. Seven means forever in love, Eight a fickle lover, Nine there will be a change of heart, and 11 means that they will be taken from you by an early death. If however, the lines were thick and leaned to the left that meant there was trouble afoot. If a pansy blooms in autumn than sickness will fill your household. If there is no rain, pick a pansy and it will come. Pansy petals are used to make a lover come to you or for rekindling love.

Parsley: (Devil' s Oatmeal, Blood of Archemorus)Is said to protect against evil, and that it can only grow if a woman is in charge of a household. Parsley signifies death and suffering and is therefore used sympathetically as a curse to sicken and wither a person of all strength.

Passion Flower: (Maypops) Gives aid to a restful deep sleep. It can be made into a tea for restless children. It is carried to attract friends and used as a sweep or wash to bring peace to a troubled household.

Patchouli: (Pucha pat) Often used to promote lust and fertility or to draw love to you, although there are those that it excites and those that it repels. Some say that it is loved by good people and hated by evil hearts, I have not known this to be the case, but more likely a test for the harmony of lovers. The oil has been used to wash dreadlocks and for perfumes. The powder can be used in money spells.

Hoary Pea: (Cat Gut, Goat's Rue) Used in spells for Money and Love.

Peony: (Woodpecker, Pentecost Rose) Are used for spells of Wealth, Good Fortune, Honor, Daring, Bravery, Longevity of Affection, Protection against Nightmares and Possession.

Pennyroyal: (Mosquito Plant, Tick Weed, Organ Broth, Dead Baby) Can be used as an insect repellant, as a tea to induce late menstruation aka abortions (BEFORE the 6th week after a missed period), as protection for travelers, to soothe tired feet, to repel the evil eye, and to cleanse and protect the aura. Be careful as many people are allergic and eating it can cause death in pets and small children.

Periwinkle: (Innocence, Sorcerer's Violet, Devil's Eye) Used as a talisman of protection, as a sweep for fidelity and to bring peace to an angry home. It is used upon the graves of children to protect them in the next life, and is used in exorcism to dispel ghosts and evil spirits. It is used to increase fidelity, love and overall passion and since it is an invasive vine to bind these things to a couple.

Pimpernel: (Poor Man's Weather Vane, Shepherds Watch) An Open flower means sunny weather, a closed flower means foul weather approaches. They are known to close themselves up in the afternoon. It is used as a protective charm against enchantments, and used to scry with because of its narcotic effects. Particularly useful in weather magick.

Pine: (Shaman Forest)Used to symbolize immortality, A Medicine Man often sits beneath a pine during a shamanic journey to connect to mother earth. A Scots pine is used at the Winter Solstice fire and is decorated with shiny objects at Yule. It is used to symbolize longevity, harmony, peace and wisdom. **Pine Sap:** (Black Salve) is used in drawing salve and to seal boats and beer casks. It is also used as protection against enchantments. **Pine Cone:** (Teeth) Often used as a symbol of fertility and to represent the pineal gland. It is burnt to bring rain. **Pine Needles:** (Spikes) are burnt as incense to dispel all negativity, pacify ghosts and dispel nightmares. They can be boiled and used as an disinfectant and antiseptic for killing germs and disease. They long ones are often used in making sacred baskets. **Pine Nuts:** are used as a food source. **Pine Groves:** are said to be the haunt of the Jersey Devil, of which there are over 50 confirmed sightings and looks like a small dragon.

Plantain: (Cuckoo's Bread, White Man's Foot, Englishman's Foot, Lamb's Tongue, Rat's Tails) Used to heal cuts and draw out infection, to protect from and draw out the poisons of snake bites and to heal and gain strength from a number of ailments. Considered one of the Nine Sacred Herbs in the Leech book of Bald. In sympathetic magick it is used to draw out snakes and reveal their identity to you; aka the people who are working against you behind your back.

Popular Tree: (Popple, Peble, Quaking Aspen, Shield Makers Tree)The buds are called the Balm of Gilead. They are dried, ground and burnt as a substitute for myrrh and in smudging. They are often used for purification, blessing, consecration and love magick. They can ng physical manifestation of spirits, and assist in soul journeys. The wood is used to burn offering for the Ancestors and the dead. The bark or seeds can be used in spells for transformation, success, shielding and protection (especially during astral projection), financial security and to fix a broken heart.

Purslane: (Blood of Ares, Milk Plant, Pig Weed) It is said to protect against evil spirits, promotes luck and love, guards against nightmares, clears the third eye, and is used as a wash for a crystal ball. Used in sympathetic magick to get someone who owes you money to pay you back and as a protective wash that promotes peace.

LETTER R:

Ragwort: (Fairies Horses, Stinky Willie, Walking Dead) Used on the graves of those who have been butchered. It's poison remains strong and potent even after its dead, and will put not only a human, but a very large horse in a stupor, and blind it before they suffer complete liver failure due to its highly toxic nature. Therefore sympathetically it is used to bring a tragic death upon a person.

Rosemary: (Dew of the Sea, Elf Leaf, Woman's Champion) It is used for love, memory, and death. Considered a woman's champion, if grown around her house, then she will rule the household no matter how domineering the husband is. Rosemary is also used to ward off evil spirits and nightmares. It is burnt with Juniper to purify the air from sickness and disease. It is used for protection against the evil eye and keeps the fairy folk from stealing a child. It was also used for embalming. In sympathetic magick it empowers the Warrior Goddess in Women and teaches them to stand up for themselves and others.

Rowan: (Thor's Helper, Sorcerer's Staff, Lady of the Mountain, Witch Bane) Useful for pies, jams, juices and wine. It is considered a sacred tree and should never be cut down. They are said to protect stone circles and the fairies. Spindles are often made of Roman and were used as wands to weave spells during battles. Rowan twigs are placed above doorways and barns to protect against misfortune , sorcery and evil spirits. It is used for purification, divination, to invoke spirits, send them back to their abode or lock them into a place (Rowan trees are often planted as borders in graveyards to keep spirits in and to protect the dead).It is burnt at Beltane and associated with dragons and Serpents which are said to guard it. Rune staves are often cut from the wood and worn as protective amulets. It is used for divining precious metals and is said to increase psychic powers, healing, success and protection. Wands and staffs made from it are protective and can raise a spirit or put it back into its resting place, as well they work as a guide and protect you from getting lost. A cross made from it and tied with red string (God's Eye) is said to be ward against witch's and evil sorcery. It is planted as a border on properties to protect families and to bring them good luck. Wattle of the roman are said to possess hidden knowledge. Its branches were burned before battle to invite the fairies to join in the battle. Berries and leaves are burned as incense.

Rue: (Weasel, Herb of Grace) an Oil tincture is used to cause abortions. It is used in gardens to keep cat's and snakes away because they don't like the smell. It is used as a holy water sprinkler in ceremonies. It is a symbol of purity at a wedding. It is a powerful herb against the laid down curse and is used as a wash to break jinxes, as a bath to break hexes, as a mojo to repel the evil eye. It can be burnt with Verbena, Mistletoe and benzoin to break curse. However burned with Lavender and Sandalwood it holds onto a lover. As a tea it attracts an appropriate mate and keeps you from making a false choice.

LETTER S:

Clarey Sage: (See Bright, Clear Eye, Muscatel Sage, Eyes of Christ) Is used as an aphrodisiac with lavender and petitgrain, It works as a deodorant and antidepressant, and is used for Immortality, Longevity, Wisdom, Protection, and Wishes.

Sage: (Toad, Wise Woman, Odin's Memory, Medicine Woman) Sage will only grow in the garden when the woman rules the home and is best grown with rosemary and lavender. It is used to cleanse and purify a space or a person before a ceremony. An infusion of it is said to enhance the memory and to promote longevity. The use of sage with mustard can kill germs on rancid meat (always add mustard to any meat sandwich when out!). It is useful in magick for increasing psychic powers, wisdom, health, skill, increasing business and eliminating grief.

Sarsaparilla Root: (Appalachian Root beer) Helps with gout, arthritis and inflammation, tuberculosis, Lyme disease, and itching. Used in soft drinks and tea preparations (often with Sassafras) or in Birch Beer. The red color makes it agreeable with honey for sweetness to use in any ritual or celebration. Also used to make health poppets and charms.

Sassafras Root: (Ague Wood, Chewing Stick, Cinnamon Wood, Tea Tree) Used to make a healing red tea. The red signifies that the drink can be used in place of mead for all rituals and celebrations, especially those with children attending. Sassafras leaves represent changes (as there are three different types) and help accepting and seeing the benefit of change. They can be used to make protective poppets for children.

Shephard's Purse: (Mouse's Ear, Mother's Heart, Shephard's Heart, Snow Drop) The plant is used to stuff health boogitys to protect from all diseases for a year. The seeds were once used as an amulet for teething infants and it is used to stop bleeding within and without. As well it can be used to kill and expel intestinal worms. In sympathetic magick it is used to remove that person whose saps your energy and destroys your cheer, but refuses to let go of you.

Snail Vine: (Bee Hive, Corkscrew Vine, Snail Bean) There are two varieties. The corkscrew is considered highly fragrant and is used in love and attraction spells. The Snail vine is considered highly invasive and is used in binding spells. Both are incredibly beautiful.

Snowdrop: (Candlemas Maiden, dew drops, death's flower)Often seen growing in churchyards and graveyards they are considered to cause misfortune and death if brought indoors. Since they are considered a very unlucky flower it is only used in sympathetic magick as a curse to bring misfortune on a person, business or a household.

Wood Sorrel: (Fairy Bells, Wild Shamrock, Indian Lemonade)Dur to their resemblance to a shamrock, they are considered lucky. Are used in herbal baths in place of salt and is said to be better than Epsom salt for this purpose as it contains salts of lemon. They make a very healthy lemon flavored drink that is good blood cleanser. In magick they bring good luck and good health.

Southern Wood: (Lady's Glove, Maiden's Ruin, Dash of Gin, Lad's Love) is used to keep moths from eating wool clothing and is hung in closets or made into sachets for use in kitchen drawers and cabinets, for this purpose. It is a good floor sweep and wash for spring cleaning to not only expel evil vermin but to refresh love and fidelity. As a Love Charm it is either put into your shoe or under your pillow so that you may marry the first one you meet. It is said to be a most bewitching herb that provokes men to multiply.

Spearmint: (Everlasting Friendship, Erba Santa Maria) All mint brings money but spearmint is said to bring money for life's pleasures! It is therefore used as a wash or sweep before celebrations and parties.

Spiderwort: (Spider Lily, Widow's Tears, John Tradescant) Said to bring temporary happiness and warn of impeding danger. The flowers only last a day and then turn into a gel. They are very sensitive to radiation and so work as an early warning system. In sympathetic magick, it represents the Spider Woman and its gel her cape. A Song of Creation is to be sung over them to create Earth Magick, Healing Magick or Growing Magick.

Spiral Root: (Lady's Tresses, Lamb's Ears, Spiral of Theodorus)The leaves were once used as a bandage. In sympathetic magick, it is the spiral root that is used to represent the universe and sending out a spell or planting a wish. The spiral goes out, the spiral goes in, so it is used for something you want to come back to you (like if you cast for love or money).

Snake Root: (Cat's Foot, Dutchman's Pipe, Naga) Once used to cure snake bites, in magick it is used to dispel curses and break hexes. It is also used to ask for knowledge and wisdom in your dreams by putting it under your pillow.

Snap Dragon: (Dog's Mouth, Calf's Snout) Is used for glamor spells to make one seem more fascinating, comely and gracious. It is also used for spells calling for deception or concealment.

Spurges: (Flesh and Blood, Fat from a Head, Snakes Milk, Milk Ipecac) May cause poisoning and blistering of the skin and is an extremely strong laxative. In sympathetic magick it is used to bring on a constant rush of diarrhea upon your victim.

Star Scabious: (Cat's Eye, Pin Cushion Star, Moon flower, Wild Devil's) Said to have the end of the roots bit off by the devil because it cured so many sicknesses. It is often tempered in warm wine for internal health. Because of this it is used for health poppets and used as a ward against disease.

Stillingia: (Queen's Root) removes toxins from the body and is therefore used in exorcism and purification magick as well as to gain psychic powers. Some believe if you lose something, you can burn this plant and the smoke will lead you to it.

Stonecrop: (Yellow Wallpaper, Wall Ginger, Jack of the Buttery, Creeping Tom, Midsummer's Men, Everlasting, Graveyard Moss, African's Head)Is considered a cure for broken and wounded hearts and is used in a bath to help alleviate the suffering thereof.

Sumach: (Tree of Heaven, Staghorn, Poison Sumach, Varnish Sumach, Poison Ivy) branches are used for baskets, leaves and galls for tanning leather, expressed oil of the seed for candles and the resin with turpentine is used for a Copal Varnish. In sympathetic magick we use is to provide someone with an itch that they can't scratch or get rid of.

LETTER T:

Tacca: (Bat Flower) This flower lacks chlorophyll and are boiled an eaten as a starch (without boiling they are poisonous). They are used as a root poppet to ward off famine.

Tamarisk: (Blood of an Eye, Manna, Salt Cedar) Aggressive and Invasive they are used to establish a building attack that can't be stopped by simple measures. The gall is used in tanning leather however in sympathetic magick since it formed by a wasp depositing her eggs upon the tree, it can be used as a Boogity heart for the spell to worm its way into being or the head as a way to worm the spell into the victims dreams via nightmares. The gall can also be used to begin a Conjure ball for cursing an enemy.

Tap Root: (Boogity Root, Poppet) The largest root of a plant, tree or vegetable. This is the root most often used instead of a Boogity as a Boogity, like a Mandrake would be for instance (but any tap root can be used depending on the properties of the root and the desired outcome of the spell).

Tarragon: (Little Dragon, Spice of Chiron) Is used as a sweep or wash in a hoe before dinner parties to stimulate appetite and peaceful or cordial conversation.

Toadflax: (Devil's Head, Devil's Ribbon, Impudent Lawyer, Plato's Gold) It is said to be able to break any hex and unbind any spell by simply walking around it three times. Can also be used in Baths and Sweeps for the same purpose. Increases money to a household by springing up new endeavors and opportunities.

Tobacco: Is considered spirit food and food for the gods; the ichar that fuels the gods and kills the mortals, a feast for the spirits. As such it is left as an offering, given as a gift to leaders, elders, wise woman, healers and medicine men. It nourishes and grounds spirits to our realm so we may speak to them (used with wormwood and yew). The thick smoke gives them power so you must never give tobacco to unknown spirits because they can hurt you, and escape or possess you. Tobacco can be used to break curses and return them to the sender. "Raise no more spirits than you can lay down" – German Proverb.

Tuberose: (Mistress of the Night, Bone Plant) Used for alluring perfume with narcotic tendencies in love and lust spells, also used for Protection. Try it with lavender and pumpkin pie spices.

Turnip: The original pumpkins, poppets, and lanterns of Samhain. **Leaves:** (Lizard's Tail) Protection and ending Relationships. **Sap:** (A Man's Bile) To kill the whooping cough, take out the middle of a turnip and fill it with brown sugar, a sap will form and this can be spoon fed to the patient to heal them.

LETTER U:

False Unicorn: (Unicorn Horn) Prevents miscarriage and averts the forces of evil in whatever manner it is used in.

LETTER V:

Valerian: (Lady's Tresses, Lady's Slipper, Capon's Tail, Ram' s Head, All Heal) The root when dried can be used under peoples floors to provide a very unpleasant stench, it can also be used in sympathetic magick to impale a victim's body with this unwashable stench. The flower is sewn into wedding dresses to protect the bride from the envy of elves. It is most used in a tea as a sedative for shell shock, PTSD, insomnia, and to reduce the symptoms of epilepsy.

Vanilla Cactus: (Queen of the Night, Torch Thistle) The big showy night blooming flowers are used to entice men to follow shades into the night only to be sacrificed upon their thorns.

Vegetable Ivory: (Old Man's Beard, Tagua Nut, Apollo's Seed) the seeds of certain palm trees that is used to make buttons, jewelry and art. Carried as talismans for prosperity, victory over evil, triumph of circumstances, peace and a better life.

Vegetable Oyster: (Goat's Beard, Salsify Root) The root (which is said to taste like an oyster) confers the sympathetic magick thereof as an aphrodisiac and can be used as a poppet to produce lust.

Vervain: (Englishman's Foot, Enchanter's Plant, Hind's Tongue) used to make an altar broom, can be carried for luck or rubbed to make wishes come true. It brings unhoped for help and prosperity, protects against psychic vampires and baneful magick, and was said to have stopped the bleeding of Jesus when he was taken down from the cross of crucifixion (it wasn't until after the council of Nicaea that Christ was made to have died, as saying so made him into a God and wove him into the web of other son gods who rose from the dead magickally like Osiris, Dionysus, Horus, Tammuz, Attis, Mithras, Krishna, etc.).

Vine: Most likely Mistletoe, Holly or English Ivy, but can refer to any climbing vine that makes it living by suckling off another tree. Used for invasive magick and binding spells.

Violet: (Semen of Ammon, Snake's Head) are symbols of mourning and love for those who have died by their own hand or their own choosing and are often put in their rooms as a tribute.

LETTER W:

Walnut: (Heart, Fruit of the Valley, Carya) Witches were once said to meet under walnut trees because nothing can grow under or very near one. Walnuts are used or carried for Abundance, Health, Mental Powers, Fertility and Wishes. They also make a very successful dye and hair rinse.

Wild Lettuce: (Blood of a Titan, Opium Lettuce, Sleep Wort) The resin or sap is collected like Opium and used for the same purpose, however is completely legal to own. The leaves can be smoked as well. In magick it is used to promote Chastity, increase Protection, bring Love, as a means of Divination, and as an aid to Sleep.

White/Purple/Black Willow: (The Whispering One, Witches Aspirin)Is sacred to the underworld goddess Hela, Hekate, Cira and Persephone. Used to protect river banks from erosion and the inner bark is collected in the spring and used as a natural aspirin. The tree is associated with death, grief, cemeteries, unrequited love or the loss of a lover. The tree is used in baskets, furniture, charcoal, brooms, doors, boxes, fodder and fuel. The Witches besom is traditionally made from three trees: The stave is Rowan/Ash for protection, the broom itself is Birch to expel evil spirits and the besom is bound with Willow to honor Hekate. Willow branches are best for dowsing for water. Willow has long been used to see the beyond as well as used in sacred pipes and tobacco blends. Prayer cloths are best tied to a Willow tree and a Wish can be made by asking the tree and then making a knot in branches and coming back to untie it when the wish is fulfilled. Tying three knots in a willow branch will give your cold to the tree. Visit the tree after a storm to ask for a branch to make a wand from and leave an offering. One that has been blown off in the storm is best but if you must cut then make a tourniquet and massage the branch before you do. Carve or cut as desired when the wood is fresh. A Willow wand increases intuition, knowledge ad assists in all magickal workings.

Witch Wood: (Mountain Ash) Worn as a necklace to thwart evil and dispel sickness. Planted for the same reason.

Sweet Woodruff: (Master of the Woods, Woodderowffe) is used as a sweep, wash and a bath to attract Money and Prosperity, Promote Victory, and Guard against all harm.

Wormwood: (Blood of Hephaistos, Crown for a King, Crone's Weed, Hawk's Heart) it is used to make Absinthe a liquor and is used with Rue as a sweep and a wash to rid the house of fleas. Crushed and put in wine from the new moon to the full moon will promote visions, aid in astral projection and assist in scrying. Burned outdoors (as it is toxic) with Mugwort it calls up spirits and can be used in spells for vengeance or to steal away a person's lover.

LETTER Y:

Yarrow: (Devil's Plaything, Nose Bleed, Old Man's Pepper, Seven Year's Love, Thousand Seal, Blood Wort, Krono's Blood, Death Flower, Devil's Nettle, Devil's Plaything) is used for Healing spells and also spells for Courage, Love Psychic Powers and Exorcism.

Yerba Santa: (Holy Rope, Gum Bush, Mountain Balm, Holy Herb) The resin is gathered and the leaves are often smoked to relive asthma. It is used as an altar offering with blessed thistle, angelica, buckthorn, and basil to makes a pleasant altar oil, consecration oil and offering oil.

Yew Tree: (The Tree of Ross, Gnarled Worms) An evergreen representing reincarnation, building a future on past accomplishments and long life, indeed it is said that the earth from beginning to end so far is only three lifetimes of the Yew (I once heard there would only be 6 lifetimes and that we are on the 5th lifetime but who is to know for sure? Perhaps I will ask the Yew myself). A Yew Tree brings lasting plenty to your yard. Staves of Yew can be used for measuring corpses, graves, the recordings of linages, memorizing long incantations, and carving Ogham letters for magickal use. Yew trees are planted in church yards and considered sacred there, in sympathetic magick they are used in spells for death, sorrow, sadness, and to raise shades and ghosts. The roots are referred to as gnarled worms and are what is used most in sympathetic magick.

The Land of Sidhe:

The Land of Sidhe is full of Arsenic and Honey; Poisonous and Sweet, Alluring and Cunning. Fairies and Brownies drinking Elderberry Wine, Make you believe that you will be just fine. Wooded paths filled with Castor beans and Mistletoe, wandering there amoung the wild forest groves. Come sample the feast of Adam & Eve, with May Apples, Wild Carrots, Winter Cherries and Corn Lilies. Mangoes and Bobbins; Cows and Bulls, will make your eyes haze and your senses dull. Soon you'll hear Angels Trumpets and see dancing Lords and Ladies, then you'll find yourself playing, Cocklebur by the Suicide Tree. Phalloidin and Lapita will offer to sing, as Passion flowers bloom in an Eternal Spring. Jack in the Pulpit will render a story of Giddee Giddee, while offering delights of Butter Beans and Indian Peas. Then Monkshood will offer you a drink from the Milky Mangrove, and soon you will be lost and give up your soul. So keep your wits about you, remain innocent and sunny, and stay far away from the Land of Arsenic and Honey! - Barbara Daca

99

10 INDEX

Note: Nothing from the last chapter (Sympathetic Magickal Reference of Herbs, Roots and Trees) is referenced here because it is already in alphabetical order.

*

PSALM - CANDLE COLOR – PURPOSE:
*

Psalm 3: Blue; Healing Severe Headache, or Backache
Psalm 4: Green; Bringing Good Luck
Psalm 4: Green; Needing Financial or Real Capital for One's Business
Psalm 5: Purple; Favorable Outcome for Dealing with the Government and Bureaucratic Authorities

Psalm 5: Brown; Successful Court Case Outcome
Psalm 6: Blue; Healing Eyes
Psalm 7: Purple; Breaking a Hex
Psalm 11 & 12: Purple; Protection from Oppression and Persecution
Psalm 22: Purple; Protection from Storms and the Elements
Psalm 22: Purple; Repelling Terrestrial Danger
Psalm 23: White; Blessings and Beneficent Work
Psalm 23: Blue; Divination and Dreams
Psalm 26: Green; Employment
Psalm 29: Purple; Empowering Through the Word
Psalm 29: Purple; Overcoming Troublesome Spirits
Psalm 30: Purple; Safety from Evil
Psalm 40: Red; Make Good Wishes Come True
Psalm 42: Blue; Receiving Instruction in Dreams
Psalm 51: White; Cleansing and Purifying
Psalm 52: Purple; Freeing One's Self from Slander
Psalm 61: Green; Blessing When Moving to a New Home;
Psalm 64: Green; Healthful Sea Voyage
Psalm 65: Green; Blessings and Luck in New Endeavors
Psalm 85: Pink; Restoring Peace Between Two Friends
Psalm 90: Purple; overcoming wild animals
Psalm 90: Purple; Protection in one's dwelling
Psalm 90: Purple or Brown; Overcoming evil influences
Psalm 94: Purple; Triumph in Legal Court Cases
Psalm 100: Purple or Red; Overcome All Enemies
Psalm 101: Purple; Learning to Break Bad Habits and Behave Wisely
Psalm 111: Purple; Charming and Lovable
Psalm 112: Purple; Increase in Might and Power
Psalm 112-13: Blue; Develop Self, Tranquility and Harmony
Psalm 114: Green; Drawing Success in Business
Psalm 114: Green, Silver or Gold; Attracting Luck While Gambling
Psalm 116: Purple; Protection from Violent or Sudden Death
Psalm 116:16-17: Purple; Safety from Imprisonment
Psalm 119: Blue or Green; Help in Speaking with Someone About a Financial Dispute
Psalm 121: Purple; Safe Travel After Dark
Psalm 126: Purple; Protection for Newborns
Psalm 127: Purple; Protect Children
Psalm 129: Purple; Empowerment Against Oppression
Psalm 142: Blue; Relieving Pain in the Legs, Thighs, and Hips
Psalm 146: Blue; Curing a Wound or Wounds Requiring Surgery
Psalm 150: White; Praise and Thanksgiving
Psalm 150: Red; Turning Sadness into Glee

The Letter R: Rabbit 1, 2, 54; Rats 57, Raven 44, Red 55, Red corn stalk 55, Red dye 4, Red salt21, Remote dowsing 12, Remote healing 15, Remote viewing 14-5; Reverse curse spell 36, Reversal salt 21, Rhymes 54.

The Letter S: Sanctification 40, Sacred sites 13-4; Salts 21, 32, 54, Salt bath 21, Summoning salt 21, Separation powder 33, Shells 54, Shoes 55, Singing 55, Smudging 55, Snakes 55-6; Southern John 37, Spirit tree 56, Spit 56, Stag 1, Stars 43, Stay with me 33, Stone meaning 5-6, Sugar 33, Sulfur 33, Sugar 33, Sweeps 36-42, Sweet Magdalene 33.

This is a List of Catholic Saints and the List of Intentions/Causes that they Pray for, when you ask them to pray for you. Listed by Causes, then Saint. Referencing the Biblical verse Matthew 18:20 If two or more are gathered in my name (YHSVH) I am there with them; that is why an Ancestor, Saint, Guardian or Spirit (Voodoo or otherwise) is assigned to the prayer as well! The following list contains the names of Patron Saints of Causes:

Intentions/Causes – Catholic Patron Saints:

Abandoned children - St. Jerome
Adopted children - St. William
AIDS - St. Roque
Alcoholism - St. Monica
Amputees - St. Anthony
Animals - St. Francis of Assisi
Arthritis - St. James
Bachelors - St. Christopher
Battles - St. Michael
Birds - St. Francis of Assisi
Blindness - St. Lucy/St. Lawrence
Bodily ills - Our Lady of Lourdes
Boy Scouts - St. George
Breast cancer - St. Peregrine
Breast diseases - St. Agatha
Brides - St. Nicholas/St. Dorothy
Cancer - St. Peregrine
Catholic universities - St. Thomas Aquinas
Charity - St. Vincent de Paul
Chastity - St. Agnes
Child abuse - St. Germaine
Child birth - St. Leonard

Childless - St. Henry
Children - St. Nicholas
Chivalry - St. George
Clear weather - St. Thomas Aquinas
Colic - St. Charles Borromeo
Convulsions in Children - St. Scholastica
Counsel - Gift of Holy Ghost
Cramps - St. Maurice
Cripples - St. Giles
Deaf - St. Francis De Sales
Death of children - St. Louis
Desperation - St. Jude
Difficult marriages - St. Elizabeth/St. Cecilia
Divorce - St. Luke
Domestic animals - St. Anthony
Doubt - St. Joseph
Dying - St. Joseph
Emigrants - St. Francis Xavier
Enemies of religion - St. Sebastian
Epilepsy - St. Genesius
Expectant mothers - St. Gerard
Eyes - St. Lucy
Eye diseases - St. Raphael
Falsely accused - St. Gerard
Families - St. Joseph
Family harmony St. Dymphna
Fever - St. Peter
Foot troubles - St. Peter
Fortitude - Holy Spirit
Gambling addiction - St. Bernardino
Girl Scouts - St. Agnes
Gout - St. Andrew
Grandmothers - St. Anne
Handicapped - St. Henry
Happy death - St. Joseph
Hazards of traveling - St. Christopher
Headaches - St. Dennis
Healing of wounds - St. Rita
Heart ailments - St. John
Hesitation - St. Joseph
Homelessness - St. Margaret
Hopeless cases - St. Jude
Hospitals - St. Vincent de Paul

Immigrants - St. Francis Xavier Cabrini
Impossible situations - St. Jude
Impulsive gambling - St. Bernadine
Insanity - St. Dymphna and Saint Christina
Invalids - St. Roque
Learning - St. Ambrose
Loneliness - St. Rita
Long life - St. Peter
Lost article - St. Anthony
Lovers - St. Raphael
Lumbago - St. Lawrence
Lungs and chest - St. Bernardino
Married couples - St. Joseph
Mental illness - St. Dymphna
Missions - St. Theresa
Mothers - St. Anne
Nerves - St. Dymphna
Newborn babies - St. Brigid
Older unmarried Causes - St. Andrew
Orphans - St. Louise
Peace - St. Nicholas
Peril at sea - St. Thomas Aquinas
Piety - Gift of the Holy Ghost
Poisoning - St. Benedict
Polio - St. Margaret Mary
Poor - St. Anthony
Pregnant Causes - St. Gerard
Prisoners St. Vincent de Paul
Rain - St. Scholastica
Rape - St. Dymphna/St. Agnes
Refugees - St. Alban
Retreats - St. Ignatius of Loyola
Rheumatism - St. James the Great
Runaways - St. Dymphna
Safe journey - St. Raphael
Schools - St. Thomas Aquinas
Separated spouses - St. Elizabeth
Sick - St. Camillus
Single Causes - St. Andrew
Skin diseases - St. Peregrine
Solitary death - St. Francis of Assisi
Spinsters - St. Catherine
Spiritual help - St. Vincent de Paul

Stomach trouble - St. Charles Borromeo
Storms - St. Barbara
Students - St. Thomas Aquinas
Sudden death - St. Barbara
Temptation - St. Michael
Throat - St. Cecile
Tongue - St. Catherine
Toothache - St. Patrick
Travel - St. Christopher
Tuberculosis - St. Theresa
Tumor - St. Rita
Ulcers - St. Charles Borromeo
Uncontrolled gambling - St. Bernadino
Vanity - St. Rose of Lima
Virgins - Miraculous/St. Joan of Arc
Widowers - St. Thomas More
Widows - St. Louise
Wild animals - St. Blaise
Wisdom - Gift of Holy Ghost
Causes in labor - St. Anne
Youth - St. Gabriel

The Letter T: Tag locks 56, Tarot Spells 62-3; To catch a Thief 30, Thor's hammer powder 34, Three for bane 56, Treasure bath 24, Troll cross 56-7; Toten Ermorden Umbringen 34.

The Letter U: UnWorting powder 34.

The Letter V: Vanaheim's Fertility 41, Vishnu Preserver bath 25.

The Letter W: Wadjet 57, Wake 39, War water 41, Ward bath 25, Warding powder 35, Washes 36-42, White salt 21, Witch ball 57, Witches Domination 35, Wood 57, Writs for Rats 57.

The Letter Y: Yellow dye 4.

ABOUT THE AUTHOR

Barbara Daca was born and raised in the Appalachian Mountains and resides in Burnsville, NC. A Generational Traditional Witch skilled in Granny Magick passed down through her grandmother. Granny Magick is the heart and soul of the Appalachia and incorporates many traditions from all walks of life. Appalachian Hoodoo is sympathetic form of Granny Magick, born and bred in the Appalachian Mountains and descended from the Vikings and Druids. You can follow Barbara Daca on her One Pot Witchery page on Facebook and Twitter. One Pot Witchery is an online and traditional coven in Burnsville, NC with annexes in Enville, TN and Tampa, FL. They also have Sister Covens in Red Oak, IA and Long beach, CA. Please enjoy our other titles on Amazon.com: The Art of the Boogity, The Art of Divination and One Pot Witchery's Stone Soup, the Grimoire of the Kitchen Hedge Witch.

Made in the USA
Columbia, SC
28 February 2022

56959263R00065